ENLIGHTENMENT...

SELECTED PASSAGES
FROM THE
KHABORIS MANUSCRIPT
An Ancient Syriac New Testament Scribed
in Aramaic
The Language of Jesus of Nazareth

ENLIGHTENMENT

Enlightenment From The Aramaic

Selected Passages
From
The Khabouris Manuscript
An Ancient Text
Of the Syriac New Testament

Translated direct into English from the ancient Aramaic with particular and painstaking fidelity to the preservation of the thought
patterns, images, and concepts peculiar to Aramaic, the native language of Jesus of Nazareth, and the language in which He delivered His teachings to the world.

KHABORIS MANUSCRIPT

Published by FHU
Printed in the United States of America

For information, please direct inquiry to:
        FHU
        P.O. Box 1009
        Grants Pass, OR 97526

Cover design: Yuri Teshler/David Font
Typography: DMI, Digital Media, Inc.

Library of Congress Catalog Card Number: 93-74380
ISBN 0-933900-18-X

IN APPRECIATION...

Gentlemen:

I am grateful to the Foundation for bringing into English imagery many of the understandings of my faith, too long obscured to the West by the nature of my native Aramaic.

Sadook de mar Shimun

SADOOK DE MAR SHIMUN,
Archdeacon

TABLE OF CONTENTS

INTRODUCTION

There is, indeed, GOOD NEWS at hand.

In April of 1954, a manuscript of the New Testament in the Aramaic language was first shown to the public in America. On that day, the Yonan Codex was, at the President's request, presented at the White House to President Dwight D. Eisenhower and Secretary of State John Foster Dulles. After their examination, it was then transported to the Library of Congress for display. In an emotion-packed unveiling, a panel of speakers headed by the Secretary of State gave tribute in an impressive ceremony.

The manuscript was labeled by the Reverend Frederick Brown Harris, Chaplain to the United States Senate, as the "N.T. Time Bomb". His words are most appropriate. We quote them from his newspaper article about the manuscript.

"The N.T. of the title stands for New Testament. More profound in its final significance than the test of any instrument of deadly destruction on the Nevada desert was a recent April scene in the Capitol of the Nation. The setting was the exquisitely beautiful Great Hall of the Library of Congress. That cathedral of learning and letters, where are stored the garnered treasures of all man's searching and striving, received that day into its custody a priceless volume, its safety insured for $1 1/2 million, escorted by motored police and armed guards.

It was about 1,600 years ago that a skillful scribe, with a evident pride in expert workmanship, laboriously yet joyously inscribed on parchment vellum the entire New Testament. The chapter headings in red are still timelessly brilliant. Across the centuries, through the varied vicissitudes of history, invasion and catastrophic social and political changes including cruel examples of man's inhumanity to man, this book has been almost miraculously preserved. It represents the canon of the New Testament on which the early followers of the Great Galilean were in agreement before divisive controversies split the church. But the thing that lifts it to the pinnacle of Biblical interest is that it is written in the language used by Jesus, who spake as never man spake, as the vehicle of His deathless concepts of life. Here are the very syllables as they fell from His lips when the matchless Teacher was here among men. It is a record to make the heart leap with excitement. Somehow, it is like hearing the One whose birth broke the ages in two, talking to our modern age without a language barrier between. Here is not a translation of the words, but the words themselves of that One who under the blue sky of Palestine declared: 'My words shall not pass away. They are spirit and they are life.' Gazing across the years to be, He warned that those who defy His precepts, which are the laws of life, will be ground to powder.

What treasures will be found as the very language of Jesus is studied can only be imagined."

The Aramaic language presents an imagery unknown to the western mind but well-known to the mind of the East. Aramaic was the lingua-franca to the Persian Empire, which stretched from the Mediterranean to the Great Wall of China for more than a thousand years before and after the birth of Jesus. The Aramaic language, unlike all other languages on earth, has no known place of beginning nor does it appear to have ever gone through any evolutionary period. It is as if it sprang to life fully matured; fully grown. An eastener speaking Aramaic could walk 4,000 miles and communicate with everybody he met. Carried upon the imagery of Aramaic, the Zoroastorian religion grew to its full flower. It is the language of most of the prophets in the Judeo-Christian faith. It is the language of Jesus. Its phonics is the language of Mohammed and the Koran. Its symbols appear upon bricks lying in the plain near Babylon which are thought to be the building blocks of the Tower of Babel, and it is, of course, the language of the famous Dead Sea Scrolls.

Its imagery and capacity for communicating the subtleties of religion after this record of use, and of success, cannot be disputed. However, its difficulty of comprehension for a western intelligence is extremely great. Perhaps this difficulty underlies the fact so poetically phrased by Kipling . . .

> "East is East and West is West and
> Never the Twain shall Meet"

The construction of the Aramaic language involves the use of a multitude of suffixes and prefixes attached to a root word so as to establish a new meaning. This is, of course, also done in every western language. For instance, we have the word "dress" and by suffix change it from one to more than one - "dresses". We have the word "man" and by prefix change the gender to female - "woman". By suffix or prefix the English language modifies the meaning of a root word in many, many ways.

In the Aramaic, however, there are suffixes which modify the root word meaning in terms of a comprehension not widely known

3

to western intelligence. In Aramaic syntax, the suffix "-oota" indicates the concept designated by the root word is then human action, active human judgment and behavior. Thus -oota added to the root word "sney" indicates malicious, vicious human judgment and behavior. The suffix "ta" indicates the root concept is a present mind set, or attitude, a force on the mind exercising a control function over what can be perceived, what can be stored in or recalled from memory and what can be used in judgment formation. The Beatitudes, good attitudes, in Matthew carry this "-ta" suffix indicating the beneficial traits recited stem from a mind set or sets, the controlling forces within the mind predictive and causal to this resulting judgment and behavior. Modern psychology has uncovered two distinct types of mind sets exercising control. One type is goals, objectives or desires, what one wants to do. The predominant goal of the moment, either conscious or unconscious, essentially controls what data the brain will select for use from among the whole supply of data always available from the five senses and memory. A second and more pervasive mind set is that controlling what is cued or triggered into use by the goal selected data. An examination of the Beatitudes shows both types of controlling mind sets, that is, goals and cue controls, to be designated by the "-ta" suffix. Thus in the translation text, the English word attitude is faithful to the Aramaic meaning of "-ta" so as to include both the data selection controls and cue controls.

With the fact of these two controlling mind forces before us, we can understand the dilemma of him who stated, "My words fly up, my thoughts remain below". Under Aramaic understanding of the mind, he had a poor attitude. Apparently he had sound goals, but poor cue controls. Thus, while his words were sound, what was being cued was unsound.

The use and meaning of these two suffixes confront us with the question of what is represented by the root word standing alone when it is without the "-ta" or the "-oota" suffix, when it is not an active mind set or attitude nor active behavior and judgment. Thus "sneyoota" is active malicious, vicious behavior and judgment; "sneyta" is the attitude or mind set productive of malicious, vicious behavior and judgement. But what is designated by "sney"? Apparently the root word to which a "-ta" or "-oota" can be appended represents a stored mental capacity, a latent, finite entity of mind, available yet inactive, a mind structure or formation developed, inherited, planted or otherwise acquired and readily available for activity. There is no English word for such an entity except the word "gestalt" applied by Wolfgang Von Kohler. The Russian Christian scholar, Ivan Pavlov, gave to the world his conditioning experiments whereby he changed, developed and reorganized mind entities, these structures of the mind.

The word "gestalt" is so harsh, however, and its meaning so fragmented in modern use another term was sought. The term neural structure was first used, but in this edition the term mind structure is employed to designate the entities, organizations or formations within the subconscious mind which are the bio-chemical electric representations of our available perceptions, ideas and capacities.

In the western mind Sigmund Freud was more than entitled to the Nobel Prize for his discovery of the subconscious mind. Apparently, for untold thousands of years before the birth of Jesus, the existence of the subconscious mind and its functioning was so well-known to the Aramaic speaking people that it was a part of their syntax and grammar.

A translation of the Aramaic teachings of Jesus into western imagery, such as English, which preserves these psychological distinctions inherent in the words actually used by Jesus Himself gives to the western mind new and deeper insights into His words. This is a new "evangelion", new "good news", for "good news" is the meaning of the splendid Aramaic word applied so many years ago to His teachings. For the first time, the western mind can easily see, hear and understand the psychology taught by Jesus.

Truly, God moves in mysterious ways. Until the discovery of the subconscious mind in 1898 there was no way for the western mind to intellectually understand the rules for sound mind development and management contained in the Aramaic teachings of Jesus of Nazareth. There is no way for a chemistry book to be properly translated if the translator is ignorant of chemistry. Unless there is an idea within the human mind, there can never be a word for it. Without the public acceptance of the science of psychology, there would be no way to communicate the psychological teachings of Jesus from His native Aramaic. One may well wonder what other wisdoms are in the "Purest Truth ever made known on earth", waiting only for us to discover the subject before we may understand that He has explained it.

Who knows? Perhaps someone has just received the Nobel Prize for the discovery of a subject which, seventy years from now, we will find has been explained in these ancient teachings.

A physical examination of the Yonan Codex reveals the unfortunate fact that both the front and the back pages of this remarkable document have been replaced with text written on paper instead of the original hide. This was a crucial absence of antiquity and authenticity since the Sermon on the Mount in the Gospel of St. Matthew was on the paper pages rather than on the hide pages, whose antiquity and authenticity were thought by many to exceed that of any New Testament manuscript then known. The particular portions missing represented an important part of the transcription of the only gospel preached in Aramaic, the only gospel which substantially all scholars, both eastern and western, agree was first written in Aramaic. Accordingly, the Foundation set out to acquire the text of the Gospel of St. Matthew in an ancient Aramaic New Testament inscribed on the original hide.

The Foundation was fortunate in securing in 1966 an Aramaic New Testament now known as the Khabouris Manuscript in which almost all of the text of the Gospel according to St. Matthew is presented on the original animal skin. No claim as to its age has been made by the Foundation, for no claim need be made. The news presented here is not the antiquity of the manuscript, but the totality and accuracy of the psychological wisdom expressed in the Aramaic syntax and concepts.

The history of the Khabouris Manuscript is unknown. It was secured by the Yonan Codex Foundation by gift from two Americans, who are thought to have secured it from the members of an ancient religious sect known to modern scholars as Nestorian. This sect is a surviving remnant of the See of Babylon of the Church of the East. It is thought by some to have been out of the library of a small church atop one of the mountains of Kurdistan. The contents of this library were seized by Turkish authorities in 1966 and now are in Ankara, Turkey, as per announcement in the Istanbul Gazette of June 11, 1966, complete with pictures of the church and some of the documents then in hand.

The language of this small church is the Aramaic as it was spoken by Jesus of Nazareth. Their script is Estrangela, long thought to be a dead and unused script since the days of the Islamic conquest. The present condition and welfare of this church and its most reverend members is unknown.

While Aramaic texts of the New Testament have been available in western scholarship since Matthew was first inscribed, all known efforts to translate Aramaic text into English have largely failed to deliver into any western language the full insights that the translator has gained from his reading of the Aramaic. This could well have been due to the fact that all western languages are descendant from the Sanskrit language brought out of the East by the Persians in their first westward conquest. Upon contact with the Aramaic, a language so much more highly developed in its ability to describe the workings of the human mind than Sanskrit, the Persian rulers adopted Aramaic as the language of their theology and the language by which they would rule their empire. The Aramaic language comprehends psychology so completely, it utilizes a syntax which portrays the working relationship between mind sets, perception, mind structures, reason, judgment, entities of mind, human attitudes, and human behavior. Also, Aramaic does not distinguish verbally between the mental and physical. The word for "near" in Aramaic includes the mentally near as well as the physically near. Nor does Aramaic verbally distinguish between a cause and its effect. The same word signifies both the cause and its effect. Such thoughts as these did not exist in the Sanskrit, nor do they exist in any of its descendant languages such as Latin, Greek, English, or any other western languages.

A new process was developed to enhance the probability of conveying the Aramaic imagery into the imagery of the derivatives of the Sanskirt without wiping out the psychological understanding implicit in the Aramaic text. In order to explain this process, a clear understanding of the nature of language should be had.

A language is first spoken before it is written, so that any language may be summarized as an organized grouping of sounds which permit thought transference between minds. Thus a language is, among other functions, a vehicle for transporting the thoughts and concepts in one mind to another. From psychological studies of the mind, we find that the human mind is peculiarly adept in organizing complex thoughts or concepts so that they are keyed or cued by a particular sound, visual or other sensory symbol. Perception of visual or auditory symbols to which thoughts or concepts have been keyed in a given mind causes that mind to perceive those thoughts or concepts, if the mind set or attitude is proper.

Obviously, if the thoughts and concepts within a receiving mind are not keyed to sounds the same as in the mind attempting to communicate with it by sound, there can be no communication, nor can there be any complex joint effort by the bodies controlled by those minds, a point illustrated in the story of the Tower of Bible.

In the translation of the Khabouris Manuscript, Foundation scholars were immediately confronted by the fact that they were attempting to set to sound symbols, thoughts and concepts they did not know. Obviously, this was an utterly impossible task.

In addition, each Foundation scholar respected the wisdom of Jesus far more than his own wisdom. However, each felt he should understand what he wrote down. Thus each scholar was embarrassed to realize that he must, of necessity, filter down the wisdom of the teachings of Jesus to a level of wisdom which did not exceed his own if he were to understand his own language, another contradiction impossible to resolve under standard translation practices.

To overcome these impossibilities, the wisdom of the ages was consulted on how best to determine the truth about that which we do not know and cannot know. In the profession of law, the rules of evidence have evolved for many thousands of years with this very object as their motivation and their goal. Consulting the learned of that profession, Foundation scholars were informed that cross-examination was the only method developed in recorded history to permit those who do not know the truth to test the veracity of communication. With this in mind, a system was devised to permit Foundation scholars to cross-examine the meaning cued by

9

English symbols which had been substituted for the Aramaic symbols used by Jesus in His teachings, in order to ascertain the verity of the resulting English text.

Accuracy, in the case of an English equivalent of the teachings of Jesus, was assumed to exist when the words of the English text trigger in the average English trained mind the thoughts and concepts that are triggered in the Aramaic trained mind reading the Aramaic text of the teachings of Jesus. Of course, the Aramaic text of the Khabouris Manuscript may not present the verbal symbolization of the thoughts and concepts of Jesus of Nazareth as He, Himself, symbolized them. However, it is a perfect certainty that no other language than Aramaic can symbolize them. Aramaic was the language of His home, of His childhood, of His teachings, of His listeners, and His language from the Cross, the language of Abraham, and of the prophets. Indeed, Aramaic is the lingua-franca of those who best taught the law behind the law.

To throw open the work for cross-examination, the Aramaic text was first transliterated and transposed into phonics, using the English alphabet. By this means anyone could identify the recurrence of a sound symbol whenever it appeared. Underneath each separate sound symbol, the idea, thought or concept triggered in Aramaic was noted. Others, not familiar with Aramaic, connected and reconnected these ideas until the resulting English text was thought by bilingual scholars to trigger the same images and concepts as did the Aramaic.

For cross-examination, a postulate was established that each time an Aramaic word appeared within the same sermon, or parable, it probably symbolized the same thought. Thus if the same thought did not appear in the English text each time an Aramaic word appeared in a given sermon or parable, a lack of textual veracity was suspected and received careful reexamination.

For instance, in Matthew 19:24, the King James version of the Bible states:

"And again I say unto you, it is easier for a camel to go through the eye of a needle, than for a rich man to enter into the Kingdom of God."

The breakdown of the Aramaic text indicates this imagery is not supported in the Aramaic text. There is no Aramaic word meaning "to go" in the verse. The word gamla is frequently rendered "camel's hair" by some scholars in translating this verse from the Aramaic. The application of the cross-examination technique described above sheds doubt upon the accuracy of this rendering. Elsewhere in the gospel John the Baptist is said to have had a coat of camel's hair. The Aramaic word used for camel's hair in that passage is not the same word as gamla. Therefore, gamla apparently does not mean "camel's hair" in this verse. Further exploration of the images keyed by Aramaic words clarifies the apparent meaning of the verse. At the time of Jesus, Jerusalem was a walled city with heavy main gates. For night use there was left open a small gate which was so narrow that only one man could pass at a time and through which a camel could not pass without difficulty and, while passing, was severely which a camel could not pass without difficulty and, while passing, was severely confined and frustrated. This small night opening, which was shaped like the hole in a sewing needle of the day, was called "kheta", Aramaic for needle. Thus it would appear that the images presented in this verse of the teachings of Jesus involved a comparison between the difficulties of a camel confined within the narrow space within the night gate of Jerusalem, then known as "needle", and a rich man confined within the narrow boundaries of the pathway into the Kingdom of God, rather than presenting the rich with inevitable doom.

In order to permit the reader to conduct his own cross-examination of the text, a limited glossary and concordance of the text is included. While the phonic spelling of Aramaic words does not conform to currently followed scholarship, it is felt to be sufficient for the purpose.

Because of the use of this method and the employment of cross-examination as heretofore described, the resulting text may be said to have been generated, not translated. Images triggered for the Aramaic mind are approximated to a fair degree by the English text presented with the exception of a few where the concept did not exist in western thought or excessive confusion attached to the usual English word. When this difficulty arose, the symbol was left in the Aramaic sound, so as to indicate a new concept must be acquired if understanding is to be achieved.

One cue or word lift undisturbed is the Aramaic symbol, "naphsha", which appears as "life", "soul", "salf", and "itself" in English and Greek texts. This word is left in its original sound, for all attempts to change it into English symbolism failed. The word is a philosophy involving life, law, cognition, physical health and the harmony of human actions and affairs with divine origin and active force. There is no word clearly cuing such a thought or concept or idea in western culture, so it is left in its original dignity. An essay considering its apparent meaning appears in the glossary.

Another symbol left in the original Aramaic sound is "rukha d'koodsha", not because its literal meaning is not available, but because of the degree of theological conflict on the concept illustrated. This sound triggers the third unit of the Trinity, denial of which is the unforgivable sin (Matthew 12:32). This is the entity which is a part of God and must be worshipped (John 4:23-24) and unconditionally loved and trusted. It is this which breaks off the effects of error and causes us to be mindful of the rules by which we should live and think (John 14:26).

With such great importance placed by Jesus upon understanding rukha k'koodsha. Foundation scholars felt it advisable to use the original Aramaic symbol. Ancient symbolic pictures from Egypt, South America and elsewhere depict the use or action of four elemental forces in the creation of the universe and all that is therein. Man, augmenting his created sensory equipment with all manner of created devices, has as yet been unable to sense or perceive any of these four forces or major energies which are said to constitute the fundamental energies creative of the physical universe and life. For instance, it is well known that the stars are expanding outward at tremendous velocities from a central point of beginning despite gravitational attraction, each for the other, which contradicts their outward rush. Some immense originating expulsive force or energy initiated their outward journey which still continues despite the contrary tug of gravity for billions of years. Man's created mind, using created constituents, has been unable to locate or contact such an initiating force, but can observe the fact it existed by observing the outward flight of the stars. After this originating expulsive force, the coalescing pressure of the gravity force acted on the originally expulsed material bringing individual units together, ultimately bringing the clouds of primordial hydrogen into the solidity of the stars and their planets. As with the expulsive force, the gravity force cannot be sensed directly by man's mind. All man can do is observe its effect and thus affirm its existence. A third force appears to operate in the physical area untouched by the sensing equipment of man. Something associated with heat appears to prevent the orbiting electron or a free electron from joining the nucleus of the hydrogen atom despite the pull of the opposite electrical charge. Perhaps that same force lifted the electron out of an inert neutron so as to form hydrogen. If so, this force is the creater of chemistry and chemical reactions and the father of plant and animal life. While undetected, there is no doubt as to the existence of this force, for no matter how low we cool hydrogen, or how many electrons we spray upon it, or how much we squeeze it, the center proton refuses to accept an electron and remains hydrogen, the beginning unit of matter as we know it. Again, man cannot directly contact this force, only sense its impact in the material world.

Rukha stands for these three forces and various invisible but material forces such as wind, magnetism, and electricity. As rukha d'koodsha, it represents man's undetectable and yet tangible force upon the mind of man, a force from God for that divinely intended for man, a fourth force which man cannot contact and as yet cannot fully perceive to exist.

Another symbol left in the original Aramaic sound is "kenoota", human behavior and judgment which we would describe as just and fair. Justness is a slightly different concept in western thought, being a finite measurable result or symptom, whereas kenoota is not only the result, it is also the cause behind the result. It is the judgment and behavior which produces justness, as well as the just judgment and behavior produced.

Another unique symbol in Aramaic is "khooba", the love we are told to have for our enemies (Matthew 5:44). The concept to be cued by khooba did not exist in western thought until psychological advances uncovered the controlling force of a set of mind. This love is an attitude, a mind set, which includes the desire for unconditional affection for the other and the cue control set which causes what is good about the other to be perceived, causes that which is fair and just in the circumstances to come to mind and causes perception of the wholesome desires and objectives of the other. Being only a mind set or attitude, khooba does not include reasoning, judgment or action, only the controlling sets which, if sufficiently maintained, fill memory with wholesome information and ultimately produce the unconditional love for neighbor and God upon which all law hangs (Matthew 22:35-40).

It is helpful to distinguish the love designated by khooba from the love indicated by the work "rakhma". Rakhma is the love for God and man upon which all law hangs. It is the love for others which produces being loved (Matthew 5:7). While it evolves from khooba and cannot be developed without khooba, mind set love, the love represented by rakhma includes reason, thoughts, judgment and behavior. If one is successful in maintaining khooba for all men, rakhma, unconditional love for all others, will develop. With khooba, the unique fact Will Rogers never met a man he did not like ceases to be unique and becomes a natural result anyone can reach. If one maintains mind set love, khooba, for others at all times, he will achieve unconditional judgmental and behavioral love, rakhma, for them as his motivation for such achievement will be continuous and his cue controls will fill his memory, perception, reason and judgment with what is good and lovable about the other until unconditional love is established.

Under ancient Aramaic understanding, the mind set, khooba, produces a particular judgment regarding another. Under modern understanding it appears to do so by controlling present perception and stocking memory. On the issue of "How should I feel towards this person?" khooba produces rakhma, unconditional love. On the question of "How should I treat this person?", khooba produces the answer of kenoota, justly and fairly. In response to the question of "How do I work with this person?", khooba produces the answer of humility, cooperate with his good and wholesome desires and objectives.

With the attention directed toward God, as it is in prayer, khooba produces a love of truth and a home in rukha. Thus the mind set, khooba, continuously maintained for neighbor and for God may be considered to produce the admirable qualities of human personality recited in the first five beatitudes.

Another Aramaic symbol not normal to western thought is "koodsha", the Aramaic ancestor of the Hebrew word "kosher". While kosher means proper as delineated by the five Books of Moses, koodsha is broader and means proper as determined by the will of God for man, both known and unknown. It represents that which is divinely intended for man.

Two Aramaic words, "khata" and "bisha", are rendered as sin and evil respectively. However, the concepts cued by these words in the language of Jesus is not normal to western thought. Each is an archery term - sin or khata representing "missing the target", and bisha or evil representing "off target", where the arrow went when it missed. Thus in Aramaic these words appear as "not right" as opposed to their normal meaning of positive wrongs. Increasingly, neural research, research into the mechanics of the mind, appears to indicate the fact that the human mind cannot utilize a right-wrong judgment approach. Apparently the mind must follow at any given moment a right-not right or use a wrong-not wrong evaluation system; that the mind's scanning system may be set to pick up what is right or to pick up what is wrong, but cannot be set both ways at the same instant. The Aramaic limitation of sin and evil to "not rights" appear to reflect understanding of this newly discovered facet of the mind's mechanics. Which of these two sets of mind should be maintained is the subject of much of the text to follow.

The limited material from the Khabouris is felt to be of sufficient quantity to add materially to the understandings available in standard texts, particularly in relation to the mind development and mind maintenance instructions of Jesus of Nazareth. The versing is in conformity with the King James version of the Bible. We sincerely hope and pray that these few lines hereafter presented will provide a wider understanding of and respect for the most complete truth ever made known on earth, the teachings of Jesus of Nazareth.

For the inevitable errors in the following text, we sincerely apologize.

THE YONAN CODEX FOUNDATION
1974

JOHN
Chapter 1

1. At the very beginning *(brashest)* there was willed action *(milta)*, and the willed action *(milta)* then was by God *(Alaha)*, and God was that willed action *(milta)*.

2. This beginning *(brashest)* was by God.

3. All was by Him and without Him not a single thing came into being out of that which was.

4. From Him there came into being a perfect life *(khayi)* and this perfect life *(khayi)* became light *(nohra)* unto all men.

5. And this light *(nohra)* out of darkness caused light, *(manhar)* and darkness did not overcome.

6. There was a man who was sent from God; his name was John.

7. This one came as a witness who would testify about the light *(nohra)* which every man would believe *(mhemnin)* through him.

8. He was not this light *(nohra)* but was to testify about the light *(nohra)*.

9. For He was to be the light *(nohra)* of complete truth *(dashara)* to cause light for every man coming into the world.

10. In the world He was, and the world was by His hand, and the world did not know Him *(yadi)*.

11. To His own He came, and His own did not accept Him.

12. Now to those that accepted Him He gave power *(sholtana)*; they will be of the children of God; those that wholly trust in His teachings *(shmi)*.

13. Unto them it came not from blood *(dima)*, not from the will *(sibyana)* of the flesh, and not from the will *(sibyana)* of man, but from God it came to them.

14. And willed action *(milta)* became flesh and dwelt *(agan)* among us, and we saw glory as if begotten from the Father, completely filled *(damali)* with heavenliness *(teyboota)* and righteousness *(koshta)*.

15. John testified of Him, speaking about and saying. "This is the true one *(hanav)*, He who, it was said, would come after me, but He is the same who was before me, because He was before me.

16. From His fullness *(maloti)* we all partook, and heavenliness *(teyboota)* stood for *(khlop)* heavenliness *(teyboota)*.

17. "While the law *(namosa)* was given through Moses, absolute truth *(shrara)* and heavenliness *(teyboota)* came through Jesus, the Anointed.

18. Man did not understand *(khaze)* God during all time. The begotten of God, He who was in the embrace of His Father, He has explained Him."

JOHN
Chapter 2

12. After this He and His mother and His brothers and His disciples came down to Capernaum, and they were there a few days.

13. The Passover of the Jews was near, and He went up to Jerusalem.

14. And He found within the Temple, those selling oxen and sheep and doves, and that money-changers were sitting.

15. He made Himself a cattle whip *(prigla)* out of strands *(khaolii)* and drove everything of theirs *(kulhoun)*, the sheep and the oxen, out of the Temple, and turned over the tables of the money-changers; their money He poured out.

16. To those that sold doves, He said, "Remove these from here,

nd do not make of the house of my Father a house of commerce."

17. And His disciples remembered that which was written, Ardor for Your house arouses me."

JOHN
Chapter 3

3. Jesus answered and said to him, "Truly, truly I say unto you 1at if a man is not born *(mityalid)* anew, it is not possible for him ɔ see *(nikhzi)* the Kingdom of God."

4. Nicodemus said to Him, "How can an old man be reborn *netelid)*? Can he re-enter the belly of his mother, enter for the sec-nd time and be reborn *(netelid)*?"

5. Jesus answered and said, "Truly, truly I say to you that if a nan cannot cause his birth *(mitelid)* of water and of rukha, he can-ot enter into the Kingdom of God.

6. That which is born *(delid)* of flesh is flesh; that which is born delid)* of rukha is rukha.

7. Do not marvel at my telling you that you ought to cause your irth *(mitelado)* anew.

8. The wind *(rukha)* blows where it wishes and its voice is eard by you but you knoweth not whence it comes and whiter it oes; in like manner, so also is every man born *(delid)* of rukha."

9. Nicodemus responded and said to him, "How can this be aused to happen?"

10. Jesus answered and said to him, "You, an instructor of srael, do not know this?

11. "Truly, truly, I say to you, that which we know, of that we peak, and that which we see, of that we testify. Our testimony you lo not accept.

12. If I speak to you of earthly things and you cannot believe *(mhemneen)*, how, if I speak to you of heavenly things, can you believe?

13. No man rises to heaven, except he who descends from heaven. The Son of man, he is a part of heaven.

14. and, just as Moses raised the serpent in the wilderness *(madbra)*, so is it necessary to raise the Son of man,

15. so that all men who believe in Him will not be lost, but will have for themselves eternal life *(khayii d'celan)*.

16. For God so loved men that He gave His one and only Son so that every man who believes in Him shall not be lost, but shall have eternal life.

17. God did not send His Son into the world to condemn people but so that there would be a perfect life *(nikhe)* through Him.

18. Whosoever believes completely with Him will not be condemned; whosoever causes himself not to believe, he has been condemned from the first, he who does not believe in the teachings of the one and only Son of God.

19. For this is the judgment that the light *(nohra)* brings to the world. Man has loved darkness more than enlightenment, as their evil deeds are from the inner beings.

20. For every one doing evilly motivated deeds hates light and does not seek light in order that his deeds will not be exposed.

21. But he that serves truth reaches to the enlightenment so that he will know his deeds are of God."

JOHN
Chapter 4

20. "Our forefathers worshipped at this mountain, but you say that in Jerusalem is where we must worship."

21. Jesus said to her, "Woman, believe me *(hemenene)*, the time comes when neither at this mountain nor at Jerusalem shall you worship the Father.

22. You worship something which you do not know *(yadeen)*; we worship something we do know *(yadeen)*, that perfect life *(khayi)* will come from the Jews.

23. But the hour comes, and has now come, that there are they who worship His truth *(shrari)*; worship the Father as rukha and also as truth, for the Father wants worshippers such as these.

24. Because God is rukha and those that worship Him as rukha and as complete truth *(bashrara)* are worshipping Him as they should."

JOHN
Chapter 5

30. "I cannot from my own selfhood *(naphshi)* undertake anything, but even while I am hearing, I condemn *(dain)* and my decision is just *(kean)* for I do not seek that my own will *(sibyanee)* be done, but rather the will *(sibyani)* of Him who sent me.

31. If I give testimony from my own selfhood *(naphshi)* my testimony is not truth *(shrara)*."

JOHN
Chapter 12

35. Jesus said to them, "A little while the light *(nohra)* is with you. Walk while yet you have the light *(nohra)* so that darkness will not overtake you. He who walks in darkness does not know where he goes.

36. While yet you have the light *(nohra)* with you, have faith *(heymino)* in the light *(nohra),* that you will be the children of enlightenment *(nohra)."* Thus spoke Jesus and went off and hid from them.

46. "I came as enlightenment *(nohra)* unto all men *(alma)* so that whoever completely believes *(damheymin)* will not stay in darkness.

47. If anyone hears my words and does not observe them, I will not condemn *(dain)* him, for I came not to condemn *(doon)* men *(alma),* but to save men *(alma)."*

JOHN
Chapter 14

26. "Now that which breaks off the effects of sin *(paracleta)* is rukha d'koodsha, that which my Father will send through me *(b'shme)*; it will instruct you in all matters, and it will bring into your minds all that I have said unto you."

JOHN
Chapter 17

17. "Father, let your truth *(bashrarak)* make them holy *(kadish)* as that which you will *(miltak)* is the real truth."

JOHN
Chapter 18

37. Pilate said to Him, "Well now, are you king?" Jesus said to him, "You said I am King. For this I was born and for this I came

24

The full color picture shown on the next two pages presents the Khabouris Manuscript exactly as two of its original pages appear today, many, many centuries after its inscription. That portion of the left page in red ink states: "End of the epistle of James, the brother of our Lord. Now the epistle of Peter the Apostle."

into men *(alma)*, to testify about the truth *(shrara)*. Everyone that
s with truth *(shrara)* shall hear *(shama)* my voice."

JOHN
Chapter 20

22. After He said this, He inspirited them and said to them,
"Receive rukha d'koodsha."

MATTHEW
Chapter 4

1. Then Jesus was drawn from *(min)* rukha d'koodsha into an
unprotected state *(madbra)* for what would be His stress from
uprightness *(adhilkarrsa)*.

2. And He fasted forty days and forty nights. At the end He
hungered

3. and then came His own temptations *(damnasii)* and said to
Him, "if you are the Son of God *(Alaha)* say to these stones to
become bread."

4. But He responded and said, "It is written that not by bread
alone does a man have perfect life *(khayi)*, but by every word
(mila) that issues forth from the mouth of God *(Alaha)*."

5. Then uprightness *(akhilkarsa)* carried Him to a holy *(kood-sha)* city and stood Him upon the pinnacle of the temple

6. and said to Him, "If you are the Son of God, cast your nap-sha *(napshak)* down. For it is written His angels will have charge
of you, and on their hands they will take you, so that your feet will
not be touched by stone."

7. Jesus said to it, "Also it is written, to put not the Lord your
God to a test."

8. Again uprightness *(akhikarsa)* carried Him to a very high mountain and pointed out for Him all the kingdoms of the world and their glories

9. and said to Him, "All these I will give to you if you will fall prostrate and worship me."

10. Then said Jesus to it, "Get out satan *(satana)*, for it is written you shall worship the Lord your God, and Him alone shall you serve."

MATTHEW
Chapter 5

1. When Jesus saw the crowds, He ascended the mount and when He was seated His disciples drew near *(kribo)* to Him.

2. He began speaking and teaching them said:

3. "A heavenly attitude is theirs *(touveyhoun)*, those whose home *(maskenii)* is in *(b'-)* rukha *(rukh)*; theirs is a heavenly state *(malkoota d'shmeya)*.

4. "A heavenly attitude is theirs *(touveyhoun)*, those mourning their wrongs *(abilii)*; they shall be comforted *(nitbeyoon)*.

5. "A heavenly attitude is theirs *(touveyhoun)*, those with humility *(makikhii)*; they will gain *(nartoun)* the earth.

6. "A heavenly attitude is theirs *(touveyhoun)*, those who hunger and thirst for justness *(kenoota)*; they shall attain it.

7. "A heavenly attitude is theirs *(touveyhoun)*, those whose love is without conditions *(rakhmanii)*; they will therefore receive unconditional love *(rakhmii)*.

8. "A heavenly attitude is theirs *(touveyhoun)*, those without fault *(dadcean)* in their minds *(b'libhoun)*; they will see *(nikha zoun)* God *(Alaha)*.

9. "A heavenly attitude is theirs *(touveyhoun)*, those serving

(abdey) the peace of God *(shlama)*; they will be called the children of God *(Alaha)*.

10. "A heavenly attitude is theirs *(towveyhoun)*, those being scorned because of their justness *(kenoota)*; theirs is the Kingdom of Heaven *(malkoota dashmeya)*.

11. "A heavenly attitude is yours *(touveyhoun)* when they harass *(radpean)* you and scorn you and deceitfully *(b'dagaloota)* speak against you every evil word *(mila)* because of being with me *(mit-late)*.

12. "Rejoice, be happy *(khdau)*, be joyful at the increase of your reward in heaven *(shmeya)*: for in such manner were harassed *(rdapo)* the prophets before you.

13. "You are the salt of the earth, but if salt becomes tasteless *(tipkeah)*, with what will one salt? For such is of no use but to be trodden under foot by men.

14. Yours is the light *(nohri)* for the world of men *(alma)*. One cannot hide a city built upon a high place.

15. You do not light a lamp *(shrakha)* and set it under a basket, but upon a high point so that it sheds its light unto everyone of the household.

16. In like manner let your light *(nohrkoun)* shine *(ninhar)* before men *(bneynasha)* for they will see your good works and then give homage to your Father in Heaven.

17. "Think not that I come to release ties *(ishri)* of law *(namosa)* or its prophets; I come not to release ties *(ishri)*, but to add to them *(emali)*.

18. For truly I say unto you, not until Heaven *(shmeya)* and earth shall cease to exist, will a letter *(yod)* or a stroke *(zirta)* of the law *(namosa)* cease to be until all of it comes to be.

19. Therefore whoever will break *(nishri)* one of His commandments *(poldanii)*, however small, and so teaches unto man shall be

27

called the least in the heavenly estate. But he who does them and teaches them shall be called great in the heavenly estate *(malkoota d'shmeya).*

20. I speak unto you because if you do not increase your justness *(kenootokhoun)* to exceed that of the scribes and Pharisees you will not enter into the heavenly estate *(malkoota d'shmeya).*

21. "You have heard that it was said to those preceding us, kill not; and everyone who shall kill *(niktoul)* causes a trial *(khayib)* for condemnation *(dena).*

22. But as to this, I say to you, whoever shall hold a mind set of malice *(eeki)* against another *(akhoo)* causes a trial *(khayib)* for condemnation, and whoever shall speak against another contemptuously *(raka)* causes a trial *(khayib)* before the congregation and whoever shall speak of another as an object of disgust *(lila)* causes a trial *(khayib)* before the gehenna of fire.

23. Thus, when you bring your offering to the altar and there you remember that someone *(akhib)* still holds a grudge against you,

24. leave *(shbook)* your offering there at the altar and go first to obtain reconciliation with your fellow man *(akhokh)* and only then come present your offering.

25. Reach agreement with your adversary at law quickly while still with him on the way, lest he deliver you for sentencing *(dayana)* and the sentence deliver you to the jailer and you be cast into the house of bondage.

26. And truly I say unto you, you will not leave from there until the last penny has been paid.

27. "You have heard that it was said to commit no adultery *(tghor).*

28. but, as opposed to this, I say unto you, whosoever looks upon a woman with lust has committed adultery in his mind *(b'libi).*

29. "Now should your right eye cause you to offend, you wrench t out and throw it away from you because it is better for you to be ess one member than your whole body be cast into gehenna.

30. And should your right hand cause you to offend, you detach t, remove it from you; because it is better for you to lose one of your members rather than your whole body be cast into gehenna.

31. "It has been said that whoever would sever the ties with his wife must give her a letter of divorce;

32. but, I say unto you, that whoever severs the ties with his wife, except for her wilful *(milta)* wantonness *(zanyota)*, causes her to become adulterous, and he who takes one so left commits adultery *(tghor)*.

33. "Again you have heard that it was said to your ancestors to be not deceiving *(tidagil)* with your oath but to fulfill *(tashlim)* for the Lord *(marya)* your oath.

34. But, as opposed to this, I say unto you, do not make an oath. Not by heaven, it is the throne of God;

35. and not by the earth, it is the domain *(dakosha)* beneath his feet; and not by Jerusalem, it is the City of the great King.

36. Do not swear by your head because you are not able to cause one single strand of hair to be either black or white;

37. instead, let your words be yes, yes and no, no. For more than this is from evil *(bisha)*.

38. "You have heard that it was said an eye for an eye and a tooth for a tooth;

39. but, as opposed to this, I say unto you, do not compete in kind with *(lokbal)* evil *(bisha)*. Instead, he who strikes you on the right cheek, turn to him also the other;

40. and he who desires *(sabi)* to litigate against you to take your shirt *(kootenak)* give him also your mantle *(martootak)*.

41. He who would force you with him for one mile, go with him two.

42. He who asks of you, give to him, and he who desires *(sabi)* a loan *(nizap)* from you, do not refuse him.

43. "You have heard that it was said to unconditionally love *(rakhim)* you neighbor *(karebak)* and have hate *(vasnee)* for your adversaries.

44. But, as opposed to this, I say unto you, have a mind set on love *(akhiboo)* for your adversaries and bless *(barkho)* him who curses you, be kind unto him who hates you; pray for those who govern you violently and persecute you.

45. Thusly should it be with the children of your Father in Heaven, He who makes the sun rise on the heavenly *(touvii)* and on the evil *(bishii)*, and brings down the rain on the just *(keanii)* and on the wicked *(avalii)*.

46. For if you set your mind with love *(makhbeetoun)* for those who have it for you, what reward is there for you? Behold, do not your publicans *(makhsii)* do the same?

47. And if you inquire for the well-being of your friends only *(akhekhoun)*, what have you gained? Behold, do not your publicans *(makhsii)* do the same?

48. Thus let your love be all inclusive *(gmeerii)*, even as that of your Father in Heaven is all inclusive *(gmeer)*."

MATTHEW
Chapter 6

1. "Look to your almsgiving that it be not done before men *(bneynasha)* in order that you be seen by them. If so, there is no reward *(aghra)* for you from your Father in Heaven.

2. Therefore, when you are almsgiving do not blow a horn before you as do those of two faces in the synagogues and public

places in order that they may be praised by other men *(bneynasha)*. Truly, I say unto you, their reward is received;

3. but when you do your almsgiving your left hand is not to know what *(mana)* your right hand is doing.

4. When your almsgiving is done under cover, your Father who sees under cover will reward you in the open.

5. And as you pray, do not do as those of two faces who dearly love *(rakhmeen)* to stand before the synagogues and in market places for prayer so that they will be seen by men. Truly, I say unto you, their reward is received.

6. Instead, when you pray, go into your inner chamber and shut your door and pray unto your Father who sees what is under cover. He will reward you in the open.

7. And when you are praying, do not recite and repeat like the pagans; their goal is *(sabrean)* to be heard because of much talking;

8. so, do not be like them, for your Father knows *(yadi)* what *(mana)* is needed for you before you ask Him.

9. "Therefore, pray in this way: Our Father who is in Heaven. Hallowed be Thy name:

10. Thy kingdom *(malkootak)* come; Thy will *(sibyanak)* be done, on Earth, as it is in Heaven;

11. Provide us *(havlan)* daily our needed bread;

12. Forgive *(shbook)* us our wrongs *(khobeyn)* as we forgave *(shbag)* wrongs *(khobeyn)*;

13. And let us yield *(taalan)* not to temptation *(nisyouna)*, but deliver us from evil *(bisha)*; for Thine is the true Kingdom *(malkoota)* and the power and the glory for ever and ever.

14. "For if you forgive *(tishbkoun)* as to other men *(bneynasha)* their wrongs against you *(sakhlothoun)*, so also will your Father who is in Heaven forgive *(nishbook)* as to you.

15. But if you do not forgive *(tishbkoun)* as to other men *(bney-*

31

nasha), neither does your Father forgive *(shbig)* as to you you wrongs *(sakhlvatkoun)*.

16. "Now when you fast do not assume a sad aspect like those of two faces who appear sad so that their appearance of fasting shall be noticed *(nitkhazoun)* by their fellow men. Truly I say unto you, their reward is received.

17. Instead, when you fast, wash your face and anoint your head,

18. so that it should not be noticed *(titkhazi)* by men that you fast, but by your Father under cover, and your Father who sees under cover will reward you.

19. "Do not lay up for yourself treasure on earth where decay and moth consume and where thieves break in and steal.

20. Instead, lay up for yourself treasure in Heaven *(shmeya)*, where neither decay nor moth consume, and where thieves neither break in nor steal;

21. for, wherever your treasure is, there also is your mind *(libkoun)*.

22. The light for your earthly life is perception. Therefore, if your perception is without fault *(pshetta)*, your whole life shall be enlightened *(noher)*.

23. If your perception be evil *(bishta)*, your whole life shall be darkened *(khishooka)* by it; if the light *(nohra)* for you is darkness *(khishooka)*, how deep will your darkness *(khishookak)* become?

24. "Man cannot follow two masters *(maravan)*. For he will hate *(nisnee)* one and will dearly love *(nirakhim)* the other; one he will honor, the other despise. You cannot serve God and materiality *(mamoona)*.

25. Because of this, I say unto you, do not burden your naphsha *(naphshkoun)* over what you shall eat or what you shall drink or what clothes you shall wear. Is not napsha greater than nourishment and your life *(pagrakoun)* greater than garments?

26. Consider the birds of the sky. They do not sow nor reap nor gather into granaries, and your Father of Heaven provides for them. Are you not greater than they?

27. For which of you by being worried is able to add one cubit to his height?

28. As to the garments, why should you be anxious? Behold the lilies of the field how they grow. They toil not, neither do they spin,

29. but I say unto you, not even Solomon in all his majesty was arrayed like one of these.

30. And if the wheat in the field, which is here and in the morning is cast in the oven, God so clothes, is there not much more for you of a little faith?

31. You should therefore not be eager or anxious over what to eat or what you will drink or what you will wear.

32. Because all these even pagans of the world need for themselves, and your Father of Heaven knows that they are needed by you.

33. Instead, seek before everything the Kingdom of God and its holiness *(zadekoota)* and all these shall be added unto you.

34. Do not, therefore, worry about tomorrow for tomorrow will care for itself. More than enough for this day are the evils thereof *(bishti)*."

MATTHEW
Chapter 7

1. "Condemn *(titdoonoon)* not so that you be not condemned *(titdeenoon)*,

2. because from the condemnation *(dena)* you pronounce *(dayneen)* you shall be sentenced *(titdeenoun)*, and with the measure you assess, so shall it be weighed unto you.

3. Why do you see the splinter *(bayni)* in the eye of your friend *(adhak)* and do not notice the board *(karita)* in your own?

4. How can you say to your friend *(akhak)*, 'Allow me to pull out the splinter from your eye', while the board is in your own eye?

5. You of two faces, first pull out the board from your eye and then you will see clearer to extract the splinter from the eye of your friend.

6. "Do not throw that which is divinely intended for man *(kood sha)* to dogs; and do not cast your pearls to the swine. They may trample them under their feet and then turn and gore you.

7. "Ask and it will be given unto you; seek and you will find knock and it shall be opened unto you.

8. Whoever asks will receive; he who seeks will find, and unto him who knocks, it will be opened.

9. Would any man among you when asked by his son for bread pass to him a stone?

10. Or if asked for fish, would you pass a snake?

11. And so if you, with your evil *(bishii)*, know what gifts are good for your children, how much more does your Father of Heaven know what gifts are right for those who ask of Him?

12. Whatever you wish men would do unto you, do you likewise unto them, for this is *(hanav)* the law *(namosa)* and its prophets

13. "Enter through the gate that is narrow. Wide is the gate and wider is the way that leads to perdition, and many are they who follow it.

14. Narrow is the gate, and narrower the way which leads to your true life *(khayii)* and few are they who find it.

15. "Beware of your deceiving *(dagalii)* prophets who come unto you in sheep's clothing, but inwardly are ravenous wolves.

16. By their fruits you will know them. Would you pick grapes from thorns or dates from thistles?

17. For every good tree abrings forth its beautiful *(shapera)* fruits but an evil *(bisha)* tree brings forth its evil *(bishii)* fruits.

18. A good tree cannot produce evil *(bishii)* fruits, nor can an evil *(bisha)* tree produce good fruits.

19. Every tree which does not bring forth good fruits is cut down and cast into fire.

20. Therefore, by their fruits will you know them.

21. "It is not every one who says to me, 'My lord, my lord', that will enter the Kingdom of Heaven but he who serves the will *(sibyani)* of my Father *(abe)* in Heaven.

22. Many will say to me in that day, 'My lord, my lord, did not we prophesy through your name and through your name clean out demonic minds *(sheedii)* and through your name perform many miracles',

23. and I will thereafter confess unto them, I never knew you, keep away from me, you work wickedness.

24. "Now therefore, whoever hears my words and then is a servant to *(abid)* them is like the wise man who built his house upon rock.

25. Rain beat down upon it, the rushing waters and blowing winds assaulted that house and it did not fall, because its foundations were established upon rock.

26. and whoever hears my words and does not follow *(abid)* them, is like the foolish man who built his house upon sand.

27. Rain beat down upon it, the rushing waters and blowing winds assaulted that house and it fell, and its fall was total."

28. And when Jesus ended these, His words *(milii)*, they were amazed at His delivery of wisdom *(yoolpani)*.

29. He had taught them as one of unlimate authority *(mshalta)* and not as their scribes and Pharisees.

MATTHEW
Chapter 8

1. When He descended from the mount large crowds followed.

2. Lo, a leper came doing homage unto Him and said, "My lord *(mari)*, if you so desire *(sabi)* you can cleanse me."

3. Jesus put out his hand, touched him, and said, "I desire *(sabi)* that it be cleansed." From that very hour his leprosy was cleansed.

4. And Jesus said to him, "See that you speak to no man, but go show your naphsha *(naphsha)* to the priests and offer your offering as Moses commanded for a testimonial."

5. As Jesus entered Capernaum, a centurion approached Him and wished of Him.

6. and said "My lord *(mari),* my little boy is in bed at the house. He is paralyzed and suffering grievously."

7. And Jesus said to him "I will come and heal him."

8. The centurion answered Him and said, "My lord *(mari)*, I am not worthy for you to enter under my roof, but only will it *(milta)* and my boy will be whole;

9. because I also am a man of authority and there are under my hand soldiers, and I say to this one 'go', and he goes, and to another 'come', and he comes, to my servant, 'do this', and he does."

10. When Jesus heard this, He was amazed and said to those about Him, "Truly I say unto you, not even in Israel, did I find faith *(heymanoota)* like this.

11. I say unto you that many will come from the East and West and will sit with Abraham and Isaac and Jacob within the Kingdom of Heaven *(malkoota dashmeya).*

12. Sons of the Kingdom will be left in outer darkness. There will be weeping and gnashing of teeth."

13. And Jesus said to the centurion, "Go, as with your believing (*heymint*), so shall it be for you."

14. And Jesus arrived at the house of Simon and saw his mother-in-law bedridden and gripped with fever.

15. He touched her hand and the fever left her. She rose up and served them.

16. And when evening came, many with demons (*deyvanii*) drew up before Him and He cast out their demons (*deyveyhoun*) with a command (*milta*), and all those that were badly afflicted were made well.

17. And so it came to fulfillment, the matter announced by the prophet Isaiah, who said, "He will take upon himself our infirmities and will bear our weaknesses."

18. When Jesus saw the many crowds around Him, He ordered that they go to the other side.

19. A scribe approached Him and said, "Rabbi, I will follow after you wherever you go."

20. Jesus said to him, "The foxes have holes of their own; the birds in the sky (*dashmeya*) have roosting points, but for the Son of Man, there is no place to lay his head."

21. Another of His disciples said to Him, "My lord (*mari*), allow me first to go bury my father."

22. Jesus then said to him, "Come follow me, and leave the dead to bury their dead."

23. And as Jesus boarded the ship, His disciples went aboard with Him.

24. And lo, a great storm arose upon the sea, so that the waves covered the ship while Jesus was asleep,

25. and His disciples gathered close and woke Him and said to Him, "Our lord save us. We are perishing."

26. Jesus said to them, "Why (*l'mana*) do you fear? Are you of

little faith *(heymanoota)*?" He then rose and rebuked the wind *(rukha)* and the sea and there came a great calm.

27. Then the men wondered and said, "Who is this that winds and the sea are obedient to Him?"

28. When Jesus came to the other side, to the land of Gadarenes, there met Him two with demons *(deyvanii)* who came out from the cemetery, so unusually violent that no one dared to pass by that road.

29. They cried out and said, "What is between You and us, Jesus, Son of God? Do you come here before the season to torment us?"

30. Now far away from them was a herd of many swine grazing.

31. But their demonic minds *(sheedii)* urged of Him, and said, "If you do expel us, permit us to go into that herd of swine."

32. Jesus said unto them, "Go", and immediately they came out and entered the swine, and the whole herd rushed to the cliff and fell into the sea and died in the sea.

33. Now those who are the herders fled and went to the city and related everything that happened in regard to those with demons *(deyvanii)*.

34. And the entire city came out to meet Jesus and when they saw Him, they begged Him to depart from their district.

MATTHEW
Chapter 9

1. He went aboard the boat and having crossed over He came to His own city.

2. And they brought to Him a paralytic while still in bed. And Jesus saw their faith *(heymanoothoun)*, and said to him who was paralyzed, "Have heart my son, your sins are forgiven *(shbegneen)*."

3. But men from the scribes said among themselves, "This person blasphemes."

4. Now Jesus knew their inner thoughts *(makhshbathoun)* and said to them, "Why do you cause yourselves to think *(mitkhashbean)* evil thoughts *(bishta)* in your minds *(libkoun)*?

5. Which is easier to say, 'Your sins are forgiven' or to say 'arise and walk'?

6. But, so that you will know that there is authority *(sholtana)* in the Son of Man on earth to forgive sins, I say to the paralytic, 'Arise, take your bed and go to your house'."

7. And he rose and went to his house.

8. When the crowds saw this, they gave praise unto God who gave authority *(sholtana)* such as this unto men.

9. When Jesus left there, He saw a man sitting in the house of the publicans *(makhsii)* whose name was Matthew, and said to him, "Come follow me," and he rose and went with Him.

10. And while He was eating in a house, publicans *(makhsii)* and many sinners *(khatayii)* came and sat with Jesus and His disciples.

11. And when the Pharisees saw, they said to His disciples, "Why does your master eat with publicans *(makhsii)* and sinners *(khatayii)*?"

12: Now when Jesus heard this, He said to them, "The sound have no need for a physician, only those possessed of infirmities.

13. Go, learn the whys. It is mercy *(khanna)* I desire and not sacrifice. For I came not to call unto the holy *(zadehii)*, but unto sinners *(khatayii)*."

14. Then came to Him the disciples of John and said, "Why do we and the Pharisees fast often, and your disciples do not fast?"

15. Jesus said unto them, "How can the wedding guests fast while the bridegroom is with them? But there comes a day when the bridegroom will be taken away from them, then they will fast.

16. No man puts a new patch on a worn-out coat lest it tear out of the coat and the hole become greater;

17. nor does one put new wine in old wine skins, lest it burst the skins and the wine spill and the wine skins be ruined, but one puts new wine in new wine skins which protect both."

18. Now while He was still talking to them, there came a ruler who approached with homage unto Him and said, "My daughter has just died, but come place your hand on her and she will live *(tikhi)*."

19. And Jesus and His disciples arose and followed him.

20. And lo, a woman whose blood flowed twelve years came from behind and touched the fringe of His garment.

21. For she was saying in her naphsha, "Even if I only touch the fringe of His garment, I shall be healed."

22. Then Jesus turned and said to her, "Take heart daughter, your faith *(heymanoota)* has given you health", and the woman was healed from that hour.

23. And Jesus came to the house of the ruler and saw the performers and people in commotion.

24. And He said to them, "Stop it, you; for the little girl is not dead, but is asleep." They laughed at Him.

25. And when He sent the people out, He hold her hand and the little girl rose up.

26. The tidings of this spread throughout the whole region.

27. And when Jesus left there, two with blindness followed, crying and saying, "Let your love act *(itrakhim)* for us, Son of David."

28. And when He came to the house, the blind ones approached Him. Jesus said to them, "Do you believe that I can bring this to pass?" They said to Him, "Yes, lord."

29. Thereupon He touched their eyes and said, "According to your faith *(heymintoun)* shall it be unto you."

30. And immediately their eyes opened. Jesus sternly charged

them and said, "See that no man knows."

31. But after leaving they broadcast it in the whole of that region.

32. And when Jesus was leaving, they brought to Him one dumb, in whom a demon *(deva)* was settled.

33. And from the moment of expulsion of that demon *(deva)* he that was dumb spoke, and the people were amazed and said, "Not even was such a thing seen in Israel."

34. But the Pharisees were saying, "As the master of demons *(devii)*, he is expelling his own demons *(devii)*."

35. Jesus was going about all cities and villages and teaching in their synagogues and preaching good tidings of the kingdom and healing every sickness and infirmity.

36. Now when Jesus saw the people His love reached out *(itrakham)* to them. They were tired and pushed to and fro like sheep that have no shepherd.

37. And He said to His disciples, "The harvest is plentiful and the workers are few.

38. Wish of the master of the harvest that he secure workers for the harvest."

MATTHEW
Chapter 10

35. "For I came to separate *(aplagh)* a man from his father and a daughter from her mother and the daughter-in-law from her mother-in-law.

36. Those injurious *(bildbabon)* to a man are they of his own household.

37. He who loves *(rakhim)* his father or mother more than me will not be worthy of me, and he who loves his son or daughter

more than me will not be worthy of me.

38. And whoever does not take his cross and follow with me is not worthy of me.

39. He who finds his own naphsha *(naphshi)* shall lose it, but he who loses his own naphsha *(naphshi)* for my way *(mitlate)* shall find it."

MATTHEW
Chapter 11

28. "Come unto me all you that are weary of labor and heavy burdened and I refresh you.

29. Take upon yourself the yoke upon me *(nire)* and learn from me that I am serene *(neekh)* and peaceful *(makikh)* of mind and you will then find for yourselves serenity *(neekh)* for your naphsha *(naphshtoun)*,

30. for the yoke upon me *(nire)* is pleasant and the burden on me is light."

MATTHEW
Chapter 12

25. Now Jesus knew the cause of their inner thoughts *(makhsh-bathoun)* and said to them, "Every kingdom *(malko)* which you divide *(titpalagh)* against its naphsha *(naphshi)* will decay, and every house and city which shall be divided *(nitplagh)* against its naphsha *(naphshi)* will not last.

26. And if Satan expels Satan, he is divided *(itplagh)* against his naphsha *(naphshi)*. How then will his kingdom *(malkooti)* stand?

27. And if I, as the prince of evil *(babilzbob)*, expel your sons

demons *(devii)*, what causes their expulsion? If this be the cause, you make them their own condemnors *(dayanii)*.

28. And if through a force *(rukha)* to God I am expelling demons, the heavenly estate *(malkoota d'shmeya)* is drawing near for you.

29. "How can a man enter the house of the strong and plunder therein, except he first bind the strong one and then plunder the house?

30. He who is not with me opposes me, and he who does not gather together with me, scatters the scattered.

31. Because of this, I say unto you, that every sin and blasphemy will be forgiven unto men, but blasphemy of rukha will not be forgiven unto men.

32. And whoever speaks a word against the Son of Man will be forgiven but whoever does so against rukha d'koodsha, I say it will not be forgiven him, neither in this world, nor in the world which is to come *(alma dateed)*.

33. Either cultivate a beautiful tree and its beautiful fruit, or an evil tree and its evil fruit. By its fruit will the tree be known.

34. Sons of vipers, how can you utter heavenly words *(tavata)* with the evil that you have? For the excesses in the mind cause the mouth to speak.

35. A man heavenly *(tava)* from his store of heavenly words *(tavata)* brings forth heavenly words *(tavata)*. A man evil from his store of evil words *(bishata)* brings forth evil words *(bishata)*.

36. For I say to you, that every malicious *(batala)* word that is spoken by men shall be answered for on the day of condemnation.

37. For from your words *(miliak)* will be your holiness *(tizdak)* and from your words *(miliak)* you shall be tried *(tithayib)*."

MATTHEW
Chapter 13

10. His disciples drew near and said to Him, "Why *(l'mana)* do you speak to them in parables?"

11. He then answered and said to them, "It is given to you to understand the mystery of the Kingdom of Heaven *(malkoota dashmeya)*, but to them it is not given.

12. For to him that it has, more shall be given him, and he will have more, and to him that it has not, so also will that which he has be taken from him.

13. Because of this I speak to them by parable because they see and do not see, they hear and they do not hear and do not comprehend.

14. With them there is fulfillment of the prophecy is Isaiah, who said, "The truth *(shma)* you will hear and will not comprehend and seeing, you will see and not perceive'.

15. For the minds of this people have become callous and their ears dull of hearing and their eyes, they shut, lest they see with their eyes and hear with their ears and understand in their minds and shall turn back and I heal them.

16. Now a heavenly attitude *(touveykeen)* is yours, you with eyes which see and ears which hear.

17. For truly I say unto you many prophets and holy ones *(zadekii)* wanted *(itargo)* to understand that which you understand and they did not understand, and to comprehend the things that you comprehend and they did not comprehend."

MATTHEW
Chapter 15

16. And He said to them, "Up until the present and even now you do not understand yourselves.

17. You do not understand that what enters the mouth goes into the intestines and after processing is expelled out.

18. But that which comes out of the mouth comes from the mind. It comes and it causes defilement of men.

19. For out from the mind man brings wicked thoughts *(bishata)*, viciousness, wantonness, lying, blasphemy.

20. These are what defile man. If a man but eats without having washed his hands, he is not defiled."

MATTHEW
Chapter 17

15. "My Lord, let your love *(itrakham)* act upon my son who has in him lunacy *(bar egara)* and often acts wildly, causing him frequently to fall into fire and often times into water,

16. and I brought him to your disciples and they could not heal him."

MATTHEW
Chapter 18

8. "Now if your hand or leg causes you to offend, cut if off and cast it away from you, for it is better *(tav)* for you to enter into your perfect life *(khayii)* while limping than to have two hands and two legs and be cast in eternal fire,

9. and if your eye causes you to offend, pluck it out and cast it away from you; for it is better *(tav)* that you enter into your perfect life *(khayii)* with one eye than while you have two eyes you be thrown in the ghenna of fire."

****

21. Then came to Him Peter and said, "My lord *(mari)*, how many times, if one wrongs me, do I forgive my brother? Until seven times?"

22. Jesus said to him, "I did not say to you until seven, but until seventy times seventy-seven.

23. Therefore, the Kingdom of Heaven *(malkoota dashmeya)* is like unto a man, a king, who wished to receive an accounting from his servants.

24. And as he began to receive it, there was brought to him one owing one hundred million dollars (10,000 *kakreen*).

25. And as he did not have it to pay, his master requested they sell him, his wife, his sons and all that he had and make payment.

26. The servant went prostrate and worshipped him and said, 'Let your spirit *(rukha)* come unto me and everything I will pay to you.'

27. The master enacted love *(itrakhim)* unto the servant, and set him free and his debt was forgiven *(shbag)* him.

28. That servant went forth and found one of his fellow servants that owed him a hundred dollars (100 dinar) and seized him and was choking him and said, 'Give me everything that you owe me.'

29. His fellow servant fell upon his knees and begged him and said, 'Let your spirit *(rukha)* come unto me and I will pay you.'

30. But he did not so will *(sabi)*; instead, he put him in prison until he should pay him what he owed to him.

31. When the other servants learned *(khizvon)* what had happened, their sense of right *(touv)* was affronted, and they came to their master with all that happened.

32. Then his master called him and said, 'Evil servant, all your debt I cancelled *(shbkat)* for you, as you wished of me.

33. Are you not obliged likewise to have mercy on your fellow servant, just as I had mercy *(khantak)* on you?'

34. His master was angered and delivered him over until such time as he paid every item of his debt to him.

35. In like manner will my Father, who is in Heaven, do unto you if each does not cancel *(tishbkoun)* for his mind the wrongs of his fellow men."

MATTHEW
Chapter 19

3. And the Pharisees approached Him to test Him and said, "Is a man authorized by any reason *(b'kul ulla)* to break the ties *(nishri)* with his wife?"

4. He answered and said to them, "Have you not read that He who created them from the very beginning created them male and female?"

5. And He said, "Because of this, man will leave his father and his mother and shall cleave unto his wife. The two shall be one flesh.

6. No longer are they two, but instead one life *(pagra)*. Therefore, that which God has created by combination man will not set aside."

7. They said to Him, "Why *(l'mana)* then did Moses decree that there be given a letter of divorce and separation?"

8. He said to them, "Moses, in keeping with *(lokbal)* the rigidity of your minds, authorized you to divorce your wives, but from

47

(min) the very beginning *(brashet)* this was not so.

9. I say unto you, he who leaves his wife without *(d'la)* a husband *(gorra)* and takes another, commits adultery, and he who takes the woman so left commits adultery."

10. His disciples said to Him, "If it be thus between a man and his wife, it is not wise to accept a wife in marriage."

11. Then He said to them, "Not every man is capable within himself of this commanded action *(milta)* except him to whom it is given.

12. For there are the faithful *(mhemni)* who from *(d'min)* the womb of their mother were born so, and there are the faithful *(mhemni)*, who from men were given fidelity, and there are the faithful *(mhemni)* that made themselves faithful for the sake of the Kingdom of Heaven. Let him who can endure, endure it."

****

21. Jesus said to him, "If you wish to be perfect *(gmera)*, go sell your possessions and give to your poor *(miskinii)*; there will be treasure for you in heaven and come follow me."

22. The young man heard this commanded action *(milta)* and went away saddened for he had many possessions.

23. Then Jesus said to His disciples, "Truly I say unto you, it is difficult for the rich entering the heavenly estate *(malkot shmeya)*.

24. And again I say to you, difficult it is for a camel in the Eye of the Needle, or a rich man who is entering the Kingdom of God *(malkoota d'Alaha)*."

25. His disciples when they heard this, marvelled inquiringly and said, "Who can live a perfect life *(nakhe)*?"

26. Jesus looked at them and said, "For men this is not possible, but for God everything is possible."

MATTHEW
Chapter 21

43. "Because of this, I say unto you, the Kingdom of God will be taken from you and will be given to a people that produce *(abid)* fruit."

MATTHEW
Chapter 22

17. "Tell us how you understand it. Is there authority in Caesar to levy a head tax, yes or no?"

18. But Jesus knew their wickedness and said, "What *(mana)* are you testing in me, you hypocrites?

19. Show me a coin for this head tax. "They then presented a coin to Him.

20. Jesus said to them, "Whose is this image and inscription?"

21. They said, "Caesar's." He said to them, "Therefore, give of Caesar unto Caesar and of God unto God."

****

36. "Teacher, which is the greatest Commandment *(pokdana)* in the Law *(namosa)*?"

37. Then Jesus said to him, "You shall unconditionally love *(tidrakhim)* the Lord *(marya)* your God *(Alahak)* in your entire mind and with your whole napsshsha *(naphshak)* and in all your actions, and in all your thoughts *(riayanak)*.

38. This is the greatest Commandment and takes precedence *(kadmaya)* over all.

49

39. And the second, which is like unto it, you shall unconditionally love *(tirykham)* your neighbor *(karebak)* as your naphsha *(naphshak)*.

40. Upon these two Commandments hangs the Law *(oreta)* and its prophets *(vanveyii)*."

MATTHEW
Chapter 23

12. "He who exalts his own naphsha *(naphshi)* shall be humbled *(nitmakip)* and he who humbles *(namakip)* his own naphsha *(naphshi)* shall be exalted."

MATTHEW
Chapter 25

14. "For instance, a man who was to travel afar summoned his servants and entrusted to them his possessions.

15. He gave to one fifty thousand dollars *(five kakreen)* and another twenty thousand; and another ten thousand; to each man according to his ability, and departed forthwith.

16. Now he who received the fifty thousand dollars *(five kakreen)* made a commercial gain *(ittagar)* from them, increasing them by another fifty thousand.

17. And so also he with the twenty thousand dollars; he made a commercial gain *(ittagar)* and there was twenty thousand more.

18. He that received ten thousand dollars went and dug in the earth and hid the money of his master *(marih)*.

19. Now after a long time the master *(marhoun)* of these servants returned and took an accounting *(khasbana)* from them.

20. He who had received fifty thousand dollars *(five kakreen)* approached and presented fifty thousand more and said, 'My master *(mari)*, fifty thousand dollars *(five kakreen)* you gave me; fifty thousand more is the commercial gain *(ittagarat)* added to them.'

21. His master said to him, 'Admirable, good *(tava)* and faithful *(mhemna)* servant. You have shown your faith *(mhemnin)* in regard to a few. I will give you responsibility in regard to many. Enter into the pleasure of your master *(marakh)*.'

22. He who had received twenty thousand dollars (two *kakreen*) approached. He said, 'My master *(mari)*, twenty thousand dollars (two *kakreen*) you gave me; behold, a like amount is your commercial gain *(ittagrit)* on them.'

23. His master said to him, "Admirable, good *(tava)* and faithful *(mhemna)* servant. You have shown your faith *(mhemnin)* in regard to a few. I will give you responsibility in regard to many. Enter into the pleasure of your master *(marakh)*.'

24. Now he who received ten thousand dollars (one *kakreen*) approached and said, 'My master *(mari)*, I know you are a hard man. You harvest where you did not sow, you gather where you did not scatter.

25. I was afraid and went and hid your money in the earth. Behold, you have what is yours.'

26. His master *(marih)* answered and said to him, 'Evil *(bisha)* and lazy servant. You knew I harvest where I did not sow and I gather from where I did not scatter.

27. It was your duty to have put my money up at the financial exchange. I would have returned and taken what is mine with its compounded interest *(ribyatak)*.

28. There, take away from him the ten thousand dollars *(kakreen)* and give it to him who has one hundred thousand dollars (ten *kakreen*).

29. For unto him who has, shall be given, unto him who has not, even that which he has shall be taken from him.

30. As for the idle servant, cast him into outer darkness (khishooka). There will be weeping and gnashing of teeth.' "

INTRODUCTION TO GLOSSARY

The following glossary of the phonic Aramaic words inserted in he text together with their meanings in English is compiled for ncreased clarification of the images presented in the English text.

abdey:	verb	serve with effect, work effectively in behalf of, produce by service, produce, bear, serve
	abdey	Matt. 5:9	serving
	abid	Matt. 7:24	servant
	abid	Matt. 7:26	follow
	abid	Matt. 21:43	produce
abe:		Matt. 7:21	my Father
abid:	noun	(see abdey)
abilii:	noun	A sect of Hebrews devoted to social truth who frequently professed and bewailed their own wrongs and the wrongs of their society.
	abilii	Matt. 5:4	those mourning their wrongs
agan:		John 1:14	dwelt
aghra:		reward, wages, earnings
	aghra	Matt. 6:1	reward
-ak:	suffix	singular, possessive of prefixed word
	(kooten) ak	Matt. 5:40	your (shirt)
	(martoot) ak	Matt. 5:40	your (mantle)
	(kareb) ak	Matt. 5:43	your (neighbor)
	(malkoot) ak	Matt. 6:10	thy (kingdom)
	(sibyan) ak	Matt. 6:10	thy (will)
	(akh) ak	Matt. 7:3	your (friend)
akh:	noun	fellow man, brother (without necessarily kinship), friend
	akh (oo)	Matt. 5:22	another
	akh (ib)	Matt. 5:23	someone
	akhokh	Matt. 5:24	your fellow man
	akhekhoun	Matt. 5:47	your friends

	akh (ak)	Matt. 7:3, 4	your friend
khak:	akh plus -ak	(see akh)	
khekoun:		(see akh)	
khiboo:	a plus khooba	(see khooba)	
khilkarsa:		Matt. 4:1, 5, 8	uprightness, force of uprightness
Alaha:		That which was before the beginning of creation. The highest, the most ultimate, most infinite, most unknowable, the ultimate source of truth, of what is, of what will be, and of glory. The word represents God throughout the New Testament wherever it appears. The Moslem word for God, "Allah", is this same word. Individual references are omitted.	
lma:	noun	world of men, world, people, men	
	alma	John 12:46, 47 (2)	men
	alma	John 18:37	men
	alma	Matt. 5:14	world of men
	alma dateed	Matt. 12:32	world which is to come
plagh:	verb	divide, halve, separate	
	aplagh	Matt. 10:35	separate
	titpalagh	Matt. 12:25	you divide
	nitplagh	Matt. 12:25	shall be divided
	itplagh	Matt. 12:26	he is divided
vala:	noun		
	avalii	Matt. 5:45	the wicked
'-:	prefix	from, with, by means of, through, in, within	

b'(shme)	John 14:26	through (me)
b'(rukh)	Matt. 5:3	in (rukha)
b' (libhoun)	Matt. 5:8	in (their minds)
b' (dagaloota)	Matt. 5:11	(deceitful)ly
b' (libi)	Matt. 5:28	in (his mind)

babilzbob: Matt. 12:27 the prince of evil

bar egara: Matt. 17:15 lunacy

barkho: wish benevolence on, bless

barkho Matt. 5:44 bless

bashrarak: ba plus shrara plus ak (see shrara)

batala: malicious, vain

batala Matt. 12:36 malicious

bayni: noun speck of grass or dust, sawdust, splinter

bayni Matt. 7:3 splinter

bey: to strengthen, encourage, uplift, comforted

(nit)bey(oon) Matt. 5:4 (they) (shall be) comforted

bildbabon: adjective injurious, adverse, hostile

bildbabon Matt. 10:36 injurious

bisha: Bisha is an archery term and connotes "off the target", evil, the result of "missing the mark" (see khata).

bisha	Matt. 5:37, 39	evil
bishii	Matt. 5:45	the evil
bisha	Matt. 6:13	evil
bishii	Matt. 7:11	with your evil
bishii	Matt. 7:17	its evil
bisha	Matt. 7:17	evil
bishii	Matt. 7:18	evil

	bisha	Matt. 7:18	evil
	bisha	Matt. 25:26	evil

bishata: noun   evil words, thoughts, acts or deeds, etc.(related to subject) (see bisha)

	bishta	Matt. 6:23	evil
	bishti	Matt. 6:34	evils thereof
	bishta	Matt. 9:4	evil thoughts
	bishata	Matt. 12:35(2)	evil words
	bishata	Matt. 15:19	wicked thoughts

bishii: plural possessive of bisha (see bisha)

bishta: An act which is bisha. The type of act implied may be inserted (see bishata).

bishti: (see bishata)

b'kul ulla: Matt. 19:3   by any reason

bneynasha: all men, the descendants of Adam, the first man with a soul.

	bneynasha	Matt. 5:16	all men
	bneynasha	Matt. 6:1	men
	bneynasha	Matt. 6:2, 14, 15	other men

brashet:		John 1:1	at the very beginning
		John 1:2	this beginning
		Matt. 19:8	the very beginning

b'shme: b'-plus shma plus e   (see shma)

cean: pure, clean, sound, free from fault (see koodsha)

	(dad)cean	Matt. 5:8	without fault

d'-:   prefix   of, in, with, by, from, who, that, which, in order to, to

	d'(shmeya)	Matt. 5:3	of

da-:	prefix	which is, that is, who is
	da(teed)	Matt. 12:32 which is to come
da-, dad:	prefix	complete, entire
	da(mali)	John 1:14 completely (filled)
	da(shrara)	John 1:9 complete (truth)
	dam (heymin)	John 12:46 completely (believes)
dadcean:	dad plus cean (see cean)	
dagalii:	plural	those who commit dagaloota (see dagle and -oota)
dagaloota:	dagle plus -oota (see dagle)	
dagle:		A mind structure or set of mind underlying a mendacious, lying, falsifying, treacherous, deceiving speech or action.
	b'dagaloota	Matt. 5:11 deceitfully
	(ti) dagil	Matt. 5:33 deceiving
	dagalii	Matt. 7:15 deceiving
dain:		(see dena)
dakosha:		The area swept by the bride's train during the wedding ceremony.
	dakosha	Matt. 5:35 domain
damheymin:	dad plus hemnin (see hemnin)	
damali:	da- plus emali (see emali)	
damnasii:		Matt. 4:3 His own temptations
dashrara:	da plus shrara (see shrara)	
dashmaya:	da plus shmeya (see shmeya)	
dateed:	da plus teed (see da)	
dayana:		Literally judge, but under Aramaic law the sole function of this judge is to fix an appropriate sentence. No judgment of innocence was possible.

		Hence a punishment is implied, guilt having already been established at a public trial (see khayib).	
	dayana	Matt. 5:25	sentence
	dayneen	Matt. 7:2	you pronounce
	dayanii	Matt. 12:27	their own condemnors
dayneen:		(see dayana)	
delid:		born	
	mityalid	John 3:3	cause his birth
	netelid	John 3:4 (2)	reborn
	mitelid	John 3:5	cause his birth
	delid	John 3:6 (2)	born
	mitelado	John 3:7	cause your birth
	delid	John 3:8	born
dena:		condemnation, sentence	
	dain	John 5:30; 12:47	condemn
	doon	John 12:47	condemn
	titdoonoon	Matt. 7:1	condemn
	titdeenoon	Matt. 7:1	be condemned
	dena	Matt. 7:2	condemnation
	titdeenoun	Matt. 7:2	you shall be sentenced
deyneen:		(see dena)	
deva:		(see deyvan)	
devii:		(see deyvan)	
deyvan:	noun	The carnate, finite entity representing an evil idea created by man, which idea is in conflict with divine design. The evil entity represented by deyvan is apparently capable of fixing or settling in a mind so firmly as to control in whole or part its attitudes, words, behavior and judgment.	

59

	deyvanii	Matt. 8:16, 28, 33	with demons
	deyveyhoun	Matt. 8:16	their demons
	deva	Matt. 9:32, 33	demon
	devii	Matt. 9:34 (2)	his own demons
	devii	Matt. 12:27	demons
dima:	noun		
	dima	John 1:13	blood
dinar:		Matt. 18:28	Roman unit of money; approximately one dollar
d'la'		Matt. 19:9	without
d'nizap:	d'plus nizap	(see nizap)	
doon:		(see dena)	
d'shmeya:	d'plus shmeya	(see shmeya)	
-e	suffix	me, my—not in possessive sense but in objective sense	
	(nir)e	Matt. 11:29, 30	yoke upon me (note distinction between my yoke, "niri", and yoke upon me "nire")
	(b'shm)e	John 14:26	(through) me
eek:	root word	Mind set or mind structure underlying the judgment and behavior we describe as hostile or malicious toward other human beings.	
	eeki	Matt. 5:22	mind set of malice
-een, ean:	suffix	renders root word plural and verb	
	(rakhm)een	Matt. 6:5	they (dearly love)
	(sabr)ean	Matt. 6:7	their (goal is)
	(mhemn)een	John 3:12	you (believe)
eeki:	eek plus i	(see eek)	
emali:		fill up, fill out, complete (see gamra)	
	damali	John 1:14	filled

	emali	Matt. 5:17	to add to them
gehenna:		Valley outside Jerusalem where refuse was dumped and where the fires of the lepers excluded from the town burned nightly.
	gehenna	Matt. 5:29, 30 gehenna
gmeer:		All inclusive. The Aramaic word for perfect is spelled substantially the same, but phonic markings indicate the word at Matt: 5:48 is not "perfect" but "all inclusive". These phonic markings were not used until the end of the first century (see masken).
	gmeerii	Matt. 5:48	all inclusive (The -ii suffix, see ii, indicates a quality possessed. Since "love" is quality under discussion, it is inserted for clarity.)
	gmeer	Matt. 5:48	all inclusive
gmera:		Matt. 19:21	perfect (see gmeer, Matt. 5:48)
gorra:		man, husband
	gorra	Matt. 19:9	husband
havlan:		Matt. 6:11	provide us
hanav:		demonstrative or emphatic phrase
	hanav	John 1:15	this is the true one
	hanav	Matt. 7:12	this is
hemenene:	hemnin plus e	(see hemnin)
hemin:		A structure of the mind underlying the attitudes and judgment we describe as faith or trust, usually faith in the true and loving God.

	heymanoota	Matt. 8:10, 26	faith
	heymanoothoun	Matt. 9:2	their faith
	heymintoun	Matt. 9:29	your faith
hemna:	noun	individual who has fidelity, faith, trust	
	mhemni	Matt. 19:12 (3)	faithful
	mhemna	Matt. 25:21, 23	faithful
hemnin:		(see hemin)	
	mhemnin	John 1:7	would believe
	mhemneen	John 3:12	you believe
	hemenene	John 4:21	believe me
	heymino	John 12:36	have faith
	damheymin	John 12:46	completely believes
	heymint	Matt. 8:13	believing
	heymintoun	Matt. 9:29	your believing
	mhemnin	Matt. 25:21, 23	your faith
heymanoota:	hemin plus -oota (see hemin)		
heymin:		phonic variant for hermin	
heymino:	hemnin plus o faith (see hemnin)		
heyminta:	hemnin plus ta (see hemnin)		
heymintoun:	hemin plus ta plus oun	(see hemnin)	
-houn:	suffix	Indicates plural, personal, human possession of antecedent.	
	(touvey) noun	Matt. 5:3, 4, 5, 6, 7, 8, 9, 10	is theirs
	(lib) houn	Matt. 5:8	their (minds)
	(akhek) houn	Matt. 5:47	your
	(makhshbat)houn	Matt. 12:25	their
	(kul) houn	John 2:15	of theirs
-i, -ii:	suffix	possessive or plural	

	(masken) ii	Matt. 5:3	whose (home)
	(b'lib) i	Matt. 5:28	his
	(malkoot) i	Matt. 12:26	his kingdom
-ib:	suffix	possessive	
	(akh) ib	Matt. 5:23	(meaning silent in the text)
ishri:		untie, unhitch, loose, release, break the ties	
	ishri	Matt. 5:17 (2)	release ties
	nishri	Matt. 5:19; 19:3	break the ties
itargo:		wish, want (compare sabi)	
	itargo	Matt. 13:17	wanted
itplagh:	it plus aplagh	(see aplagh)	
itrakhim,			
itrakham:	it plus rakhim	(see rakhim)	
ittagar:	it plus tagar	make a commercial gain, increase or profit (see tagir)	
kadish:		(see koodsha)	
	kadish	John 17:17	make holy
kadmaya:	noun	first precedent	
	kadmaya	Matt.22:38	takes precedence over
kakreen:	noun	unit of money, approximately $10,000	
	kakreen	Matt. 18:24; 25:15, 16, 20, 22, 24, 28	$10,000
kareb:		neighbors, members of the neighbor-hood, those in proximity. Physical and mental closeness is the principal element of the word. Also included is the operating self. Thus, neighbor in text disignates not only others of	

whom one is aware or near but also operating self.

	kribo	Matt. 5:1	draw near
	karebak	Matt. 5:43	your neighbor
	karebak	Matt. 22:39	your neighbor
karebak:	kareb plus ak	(see kareb)	
karita:	noun	wooden beam, plank, board	
	karita	Matt. 7:3	board

kean, keen: The mind structure underlying the attitude, judgment and behavior we describe as just or fair between man and his fellow man.

	kean	John 5:30	just
	kenoota	Matt. 5:6, 10	justness
	kenootokhoun	Matt. 5:20	justness
	keanii	Matt. 5:45	the just

kenoota: kean plus -oota (see kean)

kenootokhoun: kean plus -oota plus ak plus houn (see kean)

khanna: mercy, compassion

	khanna	Matt. 9:13	mercy
	khantak	Matt. 18:33	had mercy on you
khantak:	khanna plus ak	(see khanna)	

khaolii: a strand or string in singular; when plural, strands

	khaolii	John 2:15	strands
khashbana:		Matt. 25:19	accounting
khashbean:		to think	
	mitkhashbean	Matt. 9:4	cause yourself to think
khata:	noun	An archery team connoting miss the	

		mark; mistake, deviation from true line, misstep, wrongdoing, sin (see bisha).
	khatayii	Matt. 9:10, 11, 13 sinners
khatayii:	khata plus -ii	(see khata)
khayi:		life; often used in the sense of perfect life or reborn life
	khayi	John 1:4 (2) perfect life
	khayii d'celan	John 3:15 eternal life
	nikhe	John 3:17 will be perfect life
	khayi	John 4:22 perfect life
	khayi	Matt. 4:4 have perfect life
	khayii	Matt. 7:14 true life
	tikhi	Matt. 9:18 will live
	khayii	Matt. 18:8, 9 perfect life
	nakhe	Matt. 19:25 live a perfect life
khayib:		arraignment preceding, trial for determination of guilt; also trial
	khayib	Matt. 5:21 trial
	khayib	Matt. 5:22 (3) trial
	titkhayib	Matt. 12:37 you shall be tried
khayii d'celan:		John 3:15 eternal life (see khayi)
khazi:	verb	see, notice, understand, comprehend, learn and accept
	khaze	John 1:18 understand
	nikhzi	John 3:3 to see
	nikhazoun	Matt. 5:8 they will see
	nitkhazoun	Matt. 6:16 shall be noticed
	titkhazi	Matt. 6:18 it should be noticed
	khizvon	Matt. 18:31 learned

khdau:		Matt. 5:12	be happy
khishooka:	noun	absence of light; also connotes complete ignorance, mental obscurity, darkness	
	khishooka	Matt. 6:23 (2)	darkness
	khishookak	Matt. 6:23	your darkness
	khishooka	Matt. 25:30	darkness
khlop:		vice as in vice-president, alternate, represent	
	khlop	John 1:16	stood for
khobeyn:		injurious acts, wrong doings, wrong in the sense of a sin which harms another	
	khobeyn	Matt. 6:12 (2)	wrongs
khooba:		mind set of love. It includes a desire or goal of unconditional affection and the cue control which causes what is good, wholesome and lovable about the other to be perceived. Aramaic dictionaries subsequent to the seventh century tend to convert the concept to renaissance love.	
	akhiboo	Matt. 5:44	have a mind set of love
	makhbeetoun	Matt. 5:46	set your mind with love
koodsha:		kosher; that which conforms to divine intent for man; root of the Hebrew word kosher, proper according to the Pentateuch (see rekha d'koodsha)	

	koodsha	Matt. 4:5	holy
	koodsha	Matt. 7:6	divinely intended for man
kooten:	noun	Linen outergarment, usually for holiday or festive dress. It is the principal part of a man's best costume.
	kootenak	Matt. 5:40	your linen shirt
koshta:		John 1:14	righteousness
-koun:	suffix	indicating plural possession of antecedent, your
	(nohr) koun	Matt. 5:16	your (light)
	(sakhlvat) koun	Matt. 6:15	your (wrongs)
	(tishb) koun	Matt. 6:14, 15	you (forgive)
	(lib) koun	Matt. 6:21	your (mind)
kribo:		(see kareb)
ktoul:	verb	kill, commit homicide. Each killing was judged for evil on its individual merits
	niktoul	Matt. 5:21	shall kill
kulhoun:	kul plus-houn	(see-houn)
	kulhoun	John 2:15	everything of theirs
l'-:	prefix	to, for, at, against; frequently indicates object of verb and is silent
	l' (Alaha)	Matt. 5:8	(silent)
	l' (dena)	Matt. 5:21	for
lak, lot:		to or against you, depending on subject matter
	(sakh) lot (houn)	Matt. 6:14	against you
liba:	noun	source of thinking; called heart in the Greek but more properly mind
	(nit) bey (oon)	Matt. 5:4	shall be comforted (see nitbeyoon)

	libhoun	Matt. 5:8	their minds
	libi	Matt. 5:28	his mind
	libkoun	Matt. 6:21, 9:4	your mind; your minds
libhoun:	liba plus - houn (see liba and -houn)		
libi:		possessive of liba (see liba)	
libkoun:	liba plus -koun (see liba)		
lila:	noun	A vile Aramaic insult conveying idea object of the insult is a subhuman, or should be considered as disgusting.	
	lila	Matt. 5:22	as an object of disgust
l'mana:		why, to what purpose, especially if verb has casual inference; with no causal inference, may be "to this" or "to what", as in a question.	
	l'mana	Matt. 8:26	why
	l'mana	Matt. 13:10	why (verb is m'malip)
	l'mana	Matt. 19:7	why
lokbal:		in kind with, in keeping with	
	lokbal	Matt. 5:39	compete in kind with
	lokbal	Matt. 19:8	in keeping with
m-, mit-:	prefix	gives causal connotation to phrase	
	la mit (yalid)	John 3:3	unable to be born
	mitelid	John 3:5	able to be born
	mitelado	John 3:7	cause your birth
madbra:		area outside the protection of city walls. Also may refer to condition where one is without mental or emotional protection.	
	madbra	John 3:14	wilderness
	madbra	Matt. 4:1	an unprotected state

makhbeetoun: m-plus khooba
plus toun   (see khooba)
makhshbathoun: inner thoughts or prompting
makhshbathoun Matt. 9:4; 12:25   their inner
thoughts
makikh: noun   humility, respectful, not arrogant,
cooperative, peaceful. The concept
is a mental quality of perceiving and
cooperating with the good desires of
another.

makikhii   Matt. 5:5   those with humility
makikh   Matt.11:29   peaceful
makikhii: makikh plus -ii (see makikh)
makip: verb   subjugate, disparage, decry
namakip   Matt. 23:12   humbles
nitmakip   Matt. 23:12   shall be humbled
makhsii: tax collectors. The tax collectors of
the day were considered most vile
because of habitual use of cruel
methods. Out of deference to our
modern tax collectors, the word
publican is used.

makshii   Matt. 5:46, 47 your publicans
makhsii   Matt. 9:9, 10, 11 publicans
nalko: Matt. 12:25   kingdom (see malkoota)
nalkoota: The human judgment and behavior
produced by harmony with an out-
side will. It is usually rendered as
estate, condition, kingdom, state
(see also malkoota dashmeya)
malkootak   Matt. 6:10   Thy Kingdom

69

malkoota	Matt. 6:13	Kingdom
malkooti	Matt. 12:26	his kingdom

malkoota
d'Alaha: Kingdom of God

                malkoota
                    d'Alaha   Matt. 19:24   Kingdom of God

malkoota dashmeya,
malkoota d'shmeya,
malkoota bashmeya:

Dashmeya is a noun, as also is bashmeya, whereas d'shmeya is a descriptive phrase. Malkoota d'shmeya is rendered "heavenly estate", or "heavenly state", relating to an earthly life. Where dashmeya and bashmeya appear, Kingdom of Heaven relating to a hereafter life is employed. The distinction is necessary, but the accuracy of its application in each case is open to question. The Aramaic words include both meanings with subtle hints as to which is the basic underlying thought, whether earthly life, life hereafter, or both, available from the phonics and context. The English words clearly distinguish between earthly life and a hereafter life and cannot mean both. The clear distinction is not authorized by the Aramaic text.

	malkoota d'shmeya	Matt. 5:3	heavenly state
	malkoota dashmeya	Matt. 5:10	Kingdom of Heaven
	malkoota d'shmeya	Matt. 5:19, 20	heavenly estate
	malkoota dashmeya	Matt. 8:11	Kingdom of Heaven
	malkoota d'shmeya	Matt. 12:28	heavenly estate
	malkoota dashmeya	Matt. 13:11; 18:23	Kingdom of Heaven

malkootak: malkoota plus-ak (see malkoota)

malkooti: malkoota plus -i (see malkoota)

malkot shmeya: Matt. 19:23   heavenly estate

maloti: fullness, abundance

| | maloti | John 1:16 | fullness |

mamoona: noun   material matters, earthly lord or master, materiality

| | mamoona | Matt. 6:24 | materiality |

mana: this with a question, an interrogatory; this or what

	mana	Matt. 6:3, 8	what
	l'mana	Matt. 8:26	why
	l'mana	Matt. 13:10	why (see l'mana)
	mana	Matt. 22:18	what

manhar: m- plus nohra (see nohra)

mara: master or lord in the sense of earthly authority (see marya)

| | maravan | Matt. 6:24 | masters |

	mari	Matt. 8:2, 6, 8, 21	my lord
	mari	Matt. 18:21	my lord
	marih	Matt. 25:18, 26	his master
	marhoun	Matt. 25:19	their master
	mari	Matt. 25:20, 24	my master
	marakh	Matt. 25:21, 23	your master

marakh: mara plus akh (see mara)

maravan: mara plus van (see mara)

marhoun: mara plus -houn (see mara)

mari, marih: mara plus -i (see mara)

martootak: noun   coat or mantle used in Arabian dress

martootak   Matt. 5:40   your mantle

marya: noun   the Lord above, Jehovah, Lord in the sense of the divine (see mara)

marya   Matt. 5:33   Lord

marya   Matt. 22:37   Lord

maskenii: masken plus -i

plus -i   Matt. 5:3   whose home

Note: Phonic dots in the Aramaic text over the second letter indicates it should be pronounced as an "a". This change in phonics without a change in spelling changes the meaning from "poor" (misken) to "home" (masken). Phonic dots came into Aramaic script around the end of the first century indicating Matthew was rendered into Greek prior to that time or without benefit of the phonic markings (see miskin)

mhemna, mhemni:	noun	one who exercises heymanoota, faith; one who has faith; m- plus hemna (see hemna)
mhemneen:	m- plus hemna plus -een	(see hemnin)
mhemnin:	m- plus hemnin (see hemnin)	
mila:		word, spoken word
	mila	Matt. 4:4, 5:11 word
	milii	Matt. 7:28 his words
	miliak	Matt. 12:37 (2) your words
milii	mila plus -ii	(see mila)
milta:	noun	willed or ordered action
	milta	John 1:1 (3) willed action
	milta	John 1:14 willed action
	miltak	John 17:17 you will
	milta	Matt. 5:32 willful
	milta	Matt. 8:8 will it
	milta	Matt. 8:16 command
	milta	Matt. 19:11, 22 commanded action
miltak:	milta plus -ak (see milta)	
min:	preposition	from, out of
	min	Matt. 4:1; 19:8 from
	d'min	Matt. 19:12 who from
miskinii:		Matt. 19:21 your poor (see masken)
mit-, m-:	prefix	gives causal connotation to phrase (see m-)
mitkhashbean:	mit- plus khashbean	(see khashbean)
mitelado:	mit- plus delid (see delid)	
mitelid:	mit- plus delid (see delid)	

73

mitlate:	mit- plus 1- plus	
	ate	because of me, for my sake, for my way, because of being with me
	mitlate	Matt. 5:11 because of being with me
	mitlate	Matt. 10:39 for my way
mityalid:	mit- plus delid	(see delid)
mshalta:	m-plus shalta	noun, singular; one who exercises shalit (see shalit)
makhe:	na plus khayi	(see khayi)
namakip:	na plus makip	(see makip)
namosa:		the law. It appears to have several meanings in the Aramaic texts as does the English word law in our own language. The following meanings are noted:

A. The rules by which we do live.

B. The rules which God intended for man (see oreta). This appears to be the meaning attached to the word by Jesus wherever he used it.

C. The rules by which we should live as expanded by Hebrew authorities.

D. The rules by which we should liver according to Moses, the Pentateuch.

namosa	John 1:17	law (D)
namosa	Matt. 5:17, 18	law (B)
namosa	Matt. 7:12	law (B)
namosa	Matt. 22:36	law (D)

naphsha:

There can be no doubt that the concept to be cued by naphsha is one of the most fundamental of all the Aramaic comprehensions utilized by the prophets.

In the Aramaic teachings of Jesus, He states all law hangs upon two Commandments as follows:

"Love the Lord you God in your entire mind, and with your whole naphsha, and in all your actions, and in all your thoughts."

"Love your neighbor as your naphsha." (Matthew 22:36-39)

The first appearance of naphsha here is usually rendered as "soul". The second is rendered as "self". The concept "soul", while of Greek origin, is a cornerstone of Christian teaching. The concept "self" is a cornerstone of psychiatry and psychology. Usually these two words, self and soul, are seen to be somewhat conflicting, yet under the Aramaic language they are the same word, "naphsha".

Clearly, the concept behind naphsha is unknown in the West. Scholars have long sought to unify "soul" and "self" without success. If the meaning of naphsha could be ascertained, the unification is obtained, for the word is the source of both "soul" and "self" in western ethics.

To assist in defining the concept it is helpful to review its uses by one who fully understood it. Fortunately, it is used many times by Jesus in the Gospel of Matthew, the only Gospel first preached and written in the Aramaic.

General familiarity with the style used by Jesus in discourse is helpful in gaining insight into a term He used, as is also some of the peculiarities of the Aramaic thought patterns. Throughout His teaching, Jesus would state a truth well understood by His listeners, and then expand from it in logical steps to make His point. With this in mind, several uses of naphsha occur which Jesus apparently felt would be fully understood by those listening.

After healing the leper, Jesus is reported to have told him:

"Go show your naphsha to the priests... "("Matthew 8:4)

Here He was using naphsha with the assumption it was understood by an ordinary person. In this use, it appears to mean the healed appearance of the former leper. It should be kept in mind that the Aramaic does not usually employ a verbal distinction between a cause and its effect. While naphsha relates to physical effect here, the clearing of leprosy, it could literally mean an underlying control of the body which caused this effect and convey exactly the same understanding.

Again in Matthew 12:25, Jesus uses naphsha with the apparent belief it was understood by His listeners. There He states:

"Every kingdom which you divide against its naphsha will decay, and every house and city which shall be divided against its naphsha will not last."

With this use, naphsha shows as the basic control, the fundamental controlling source of life for a city, a house or a kingdom. Here the word appears related to a controlling source or cause and not to its effect. The breadth and scope of the controlling cause, the life force of the city, house or kingdom designated by naphsha seems to be total, for to run counter to it is death for a city, house or kingdom. In Matthew 9:21, it is stated by the writer of the Gospel with the apparent belief he would be understood, that a woman desiring to be healed of a twelve-year flow of blood, was saying in her naphsha, "Even if I only touch the fringe of His garment, I shall be healed". Immediately thereafter, she did exactly what she was saying in her "naphsha", indicating the set or goal within her naphsha controlled her behavior.

From the Aramaic Gospel of John, which was first stated in the Greek, the concept "will" is tied to naphsha with these words attributed to Jesus:

"I cannot from my own selfhood (naphsha) undertake anything, but even while I am hearing, I condemn and my decision is just for I do not seek that my will be served, but rather the will of Him who sent me." (John 5:30)

Clearly, there is in this statement recognition of naphsha as the source of control for judgment and comprehension, but not an initiating control. Also indicated, is the fact that naphsha is subservient and must yield or alter its effect to conform to a person's will, a person's goals.

From the above uses it is abundantly clear that naphsha, at the time of Jesus, was generally understood as the control entity behind the physical, mental and behaving self. With the unification of cause and effect implicit in Aramaic and the unification of a control source for the mental and the physical implicit in these uses, naphsha, therefore, stands for all mental and physical conditions and the control source of mental and physical development. This span of meaning lays the basis for its translations into the varied English words, "soul", "self", "itself" and "life".

Also, it may be noted that there is in the above quoted uses the implied suggestion that naphsha may have a quality of performance meaning. With the leper, the instruction to show his naphsha suggests his naphsha might have changed for the better, or might have improved its performance. With respect to the naphsha of the city, house and kingdom, an implication of correctness, of truth in addition to controlling power, envelopes the meaning of the words. This implication of quality of effect, but mixed with an intrinsic tie to truth, is borne out in other statements, but these are instructional statements of Jesus, apparently intended to inform, to teach, rather than to communicate through use of a mutually understood term.

In Matthew 6:25, the quality of performance, fact of control and tie to truth elements of naphsha, all appear where He gives instructions on making things easier for naphsha:

"Do not burden your naphsha over what you shall eat or what you shall drink or what clothes you shall wear. Is not naphsha greater than nourishment, and your life greater than garments?"

In line with the thought of Matthew 6:25, He indicates in Matthew 6:33 the results achieved by naphsha varies in conformity with the propriety of an individual's goal or set of will, where in Matthew 6:33 He states:

"Seek before everything the Kingdom of God."

This implication, that naphsha, if it is to function properly, must be accompanied by a proper alignment of human will, is in no way denied by any of the communicating uses of the word.

In Matthew 11:29, He states:

"Take upon yourself the yoke upon me and learn from me that I am serene and peaceful in mind, and you will find for yourself serenity for your naphsha."

This is an instructional speech and indicates one's naphsha may experience unnecessary difficulty and conflict unless will and goals be conformed to certain rules or guidelines. However, there is no suggestion here that a naphsha with burdens is less a naphsha than one without burdens.

In Matthew 10:39, it is indicated that a naphsha operating without these certain guidelines shall cease to operate as naphsha. There He states:

"He who finds his own naphsha shall lose it, but he who loses his own naphsha for my way shall find it."

In comprehending this passage, it should be kept in mind that Aramaic offers no distinction between a cause and its effect. The finding and losing may be construed as losing the effect of naphsha and gaining the effect of naphsha.

To lose the effect of one's naphsha, then, appears to be the result of that naphsha is itself not under a will serving proper guidelines. However, it should be noted that nothing so far indicates positively that one's naphsha or a city's naphsha is destroyed by any such failure. Instead, it would appear that its effect may be lost causing difficulties of a physical or mental nature if there be no proper conformity of will, but the entity itself would appear to continue to exist, even though disconnected from control and contact with "self". Thus, the quality implications surrounding these uses of the word naphsha appear to relate not so much to the quality of the entity as to its achieved results, with the case of a poor naphsha reflecting not so much the quality of the entity as to its achieved results. The cause of poor results is laid not to a poor quality naphsha but to an improper will or goal.

In Matthew 23:12, we see another instructional section on the concept naphsha. There He states:

"He who exalts his naphsha shall be humbled, and he who humbles his own naphsha shall be exalted."

Clearly, in this instruction, the quality of human performance is directly tied to the quality of what is willed over naphsha, that fundamental organizing and controlling core to mind and body.

These instances of the use of the Aramaic concept naphsha by one who well understood its meaning give us a fairly precise understanding of the term.

Naphsha is the controlling core, the managing agent, the source of physical and mental development, and may be used to designate the results of its operation. The term may be applied to any functioning entity involving human beings, as, for instance, a house, city or country. While every human has a naphsha by virtue of his existence, the results achieved by this controlling entity will be impaired by its subordination to an improper will, in which event behavior, ideation and physical well-being shall deteriorate.

Looking into the realm of psychology, a few points can now be clarified with respect to this control entity for humans and human endeavor. Naphsha apparently can control the mind and body which are themselves largely controlled at the subconscious level. Naphsha is, therefore, located within the unconscious, below and behind and directly controlling functions of the subconscious. This is, of course, an absolute necessity from a time sequence standpoint if naphsha participated in the physical formation of the subconscious, as is implied in the above uses of the term.

Hence, being a part of the lower unconscious, it is not usually capable of direct contact with our reasoning minds nor can our reasoning minds directly contact it.

Naphsha cannot execute its natural control function properly if the controlling will is not harmonious with proper guidelines. It would, however, produce quality results with mind and body if the controlling will is harmonious with proper guidelines.

The fact of rukha d'koodsha exerting its outward force in harmony with divine will and human desires exerting their force inward generates an interface where they meet if the two sets of forces are not in harmony. What is scribed or formed upon that interface within a human mind is a history of its life. Scribing truly so as to harmonize the whole mind and man's desires with the rukha force is, theologically speaking, the purpose of human life. Man can no more sense or directly contact this rukha force within him with his instruments than he can contact the three creative forces whose impact in the physical world may be noted (see Introduction). In fact man appears to have difficulty sensing the existence of rukha d'koodsha in human life.

naphshi	John 5:30, 31	my own selfhood
naphshak	Matt. 4:6	your naphsha
naphshkoun	Matt. 6:25	your naphsha
naphsha	Matt. 6:25	naphsha
naphshak	Matt. 8:4	your naphsha
naphshi	Matt. 10:39 (2)	his own naphsha
naphshtoun	Matt. 11:29	your naphsha
naphshi	Matt: 12:25 (3)	its naphsha
naphshi	Matt. 12:26	his naphsha
naphshak	Matt. 22:37, 39	your naphsha
naphshi	Matt. 23:12 (2)	his naphsha

	(Note the distinction in the meaning of naphsha in a translation from the Greek and the use of naphsha in the Aramaic Gospel of Matthew.)		
naphshi:	naphsha plus -i (see naphsha)		
naphshkoun:	naphsha plus		
	-koun	(see naphsha)	
naphshak:	naphsha plus -ak (see naphsha)		
naphshtoun:	naphsha plus		
	-toun	(see naphsha)	
nartoun:	verb	earn, gain	
	nartoun	Matt. 5:5	will gain
ne-:	prefix	again, short form of netri, twice	
	ne (telid)	John 3:4 (2)	re (born)
neekh:		rest, repose, serene	
	neekh	Matt. 11:29	serene
	neekh	Matt. 11:29	serenity
netelid:	ne-(netri) plus		
	delid	(see delid)	
ni-, nit-:	prefix	indicates future tense	
	ni (khzi)	John 3:3	to see
	nit (beyoon)	Matt. 5:4	shall (be comforted)
	ni (khazoun)	Matt. 5:8	will (see)
	ni (ktoul)	Matt. 5:21	shall (kill)
	ni (shbook)	Matt. 6:14	will (forgive)
	ni (snee)	Matt. 6:24	will (hate)
	ni(rakhim)	Matt. 6:24	will (dearly love)
	nit (plagh)	Matt. 12:25	shall (be divided)
nikhzi:	nit- plus khazi (see khazi)		
nikhazoun:	ni-plus khazi		
	plus -oun	(see khazi)	

niktoul:	ni-plus ktoul	(see ktoul)
ninbar:		
(nanhar):	ninhar	Matt. 5:16 shine
nire:		yoke, ties, service (plus e)
	nire	Matt. 11:29 yoke upon me
nirakhim:	ni- plus rakhim (see rakhim)	
nishbook:	ni-plus shbag	(see shbag)
nisnee:	ni-plus snee	(see snee)
nisyouna:	noun	temptation
	nisyouna	Matt. 6:13 temptation
nitbeyoon:	nit-plus liba	The idea or thought represented by
	plus -oon	this word is actually 'shall be cured

of mental stress'. There is no word
or symbol in the English to convey
the idea of freedom from mental
stress. The word "comforted" is
used for nitbeyoon for lack of an
appropriate term. (see Matt. 5:4)

nitmakip:	nit-plus makip humbled (see makip)	
nitplagh:	nit-plus aplagh (see aplagh)	
nizap:		loan, borrowing
	nizap	Matt. 5:42 loan
noher:		(see nohra)
nohra:		light, enlightenment. The Aramaic

idiom often equates light with
knowledge, darkness with ignorance,
and sight with understanding.

	nohra	John 1:4, 5, 7
		8 (2), 9 light
	manhar	John 1:5 caused light
	nohra	John 3:19 light

	nohra	John 12:35 (2)	light
	nohra	John 12:36 (2)	light
	nohra	John 12:36, 46	enlightenment
	nohri	Matt. 5:14	yours is the light
	nohrkoun	Matt. 5:16	your light
	noher	Matt. 6:22	enlightened
	nohra	Matt. 6:23	light
nohrkoun:	nohra plus -koun (see nohra)		
-oon, -oun:	suffix	plural subject, personal for antecedent verb	
	(nitbey) oon	Matt. 5:4	they
	(nart) oun	Matt. 5:5	they
	(nikhaz) oun	Matt. 5:8	they
	(tishbk) oun	Matt. 6:14	(you will forgive) them
	(mitkhaz) oun	Matt. 6:16	(shall be noticed)
-oota:	suffix	designates that a mind set or attitude has controlled perception, reason and memory and is now lifted in function from a control set to physical action or decided judgment.	
	(teyb)oota	John 1:14, 16 (2), 17	heavenliness
	(ken)oota	Matt. 5:6	just behavior
	(b'dagal) oota	Matt. 5:11	deceitful(ly)
	(heyman) oota	Matt. 8:10	faith (a fixed judgment)
oreta:	noun	from the same root as Torah; often designates the Pentateuch or Law of Moses. Oreta is an Aramaic word as opposed to namosa which is a word of Greek origin. The Pentateuch designated the Law God intended for man. (see namosa-B)	

	oreta	Matt. 22:40 law (same as namosa-B)
pagra:	noun	mortal body, earthly life, life
	pagrakoun	Matt. 6:25 your life
	pagra	Matt. 19:6 life
paracleta:		either a Greek or Persian term. If Persian, it is paric plus leta. Paric in Persian is break loose, break away. Leta means the curse of, effects of error or sin. Thus the combination is rendered "that which breaks off the effects of sin". The Persian choice is selected.
	paracleta	John 14:26 that which breaks off the effects of sin
pokdanii:		commandments, mandates
	pokdanii	Matt. 5:19 commandments
	pokdana	Matt. 22:36 commandment
prigla:	noun	pitchfork, broom or instrument for controlling draft animals, cattle whip
	prigla	John 2:15 cattle whip
pshetta:		true, without fault
	pshetta	Matt. 6:22 without fault
radpean:		harass
	radpean	Matt. 5:11 harass
	rdapo	Matt. 5:12 were harassed
raka:	noun	Aramaic insult implying object is a contemptible person, unworthy of respect.
	raka	Matt. 5:22 speak contemptuously
rakhma:		the love upon which law hangs;

		unconditional love; love without request or demand for a reward or return; pure love which includes reason, judgment and behavior (see khooba)	
	rakhmanii	Matt. 5:7	whose love is without conditions
	rakhmii	Matt. 5:7	unconditional love
	rakhim	Matt. 5:43	to unconditionally love
	rakhmeen	Matt. 6:5	dearly love
	nirakhim	Matt. 6:24	will dearly love
	itrakhim	Matt. 9:27	let your love act
	itrakham	Matt. 9:36	love reached out
	rakhim	Matt. 10:37	loves
	itrakham	Matt 17:15	let your love act
	itrakhim	Matt.18:27	enacted love
	tidrakhim	Matt. 22:37	you shall unconditionally love
	tirkham	Matt. 22:39	you shall unconditionally love

rakhmanii: (see rakhma).

rakhmeen: rakhim plus -een (see rakhma)

rakhmii: (see rakhma)

rdapo: (see radpean)

riayana: noun   source of thought, thoughts
riayanak   Matt. 22:37   your thoughts

ribyatak: ribyat plus -ak Matt. 25:27   to compound interest

rukh: Matt. 5:3   a phonic variant or rukha

rukha: spirit, energy, wind, electricity. There is always the quality of a

		"force" in this word. Where	
the		"force" is rukha d'koodsha,	
the third		unit of the Trinity, it is left	
untrans-		lated.	
	rukha	John 3:5, 6, 8	
	rukha	John 3:8	wind
	rukha	John 4:23, 24 (2)	
	rukha	Matt. 8:26	wind
	rukha	Matt. 12:28	force
	rukha	Matt. 12:31	
	rukha	Matt. 18:26, 29 spirit	
rukha d'koodsha:		Lit: force for that which is divinely intended for man; the third unit of the Trinity	
	rukha d'koodsha John 14:26; 20:22		
	rukha d'koodsha Matt. 4:1; 12:32		
sabi:		wish, intend, will, desire (establish goal, set an objective)	
	sabi	Matt. 5:40	desire
	sabi	Matt. 5:42	desires
	sabrean	Matt. 6:7	their goal is
	sabi	Matt. 8:2, 3	desire
	sabi	Matt. 18:30	will
sabrean:	sabi plus -ean (see sabi)		
satana:	descriptive noun the absence of good		
	satana	Matt. 4:10	satan
shalit:	noun	act of ultimate executive authority. A dictator would be called shultanna.	
	mshalta	Matt. 7:29	one of ultimate authority
shama:		John 18:37	hear

shapera:	adjective	beautiful, becoming	
	shapera	Matt. 7:17	beautiful
shbag:	verb	cancel, forgive, leave	
	shbook	Matt. 5:24	leave
	shbook	Matt. 6:12	forgive
	shbag	Matt. 6:12	forgave
	tishbkoun	Matt. 6:14, 15	you forgive
	nishbook	Matt. 6:14	will forgive
	shbig	Matt. 6:15	does forgive
	shbegneen	Matt. 9:2	forgiven
	shbag	Matt. 18:27	cancelled
	shbkat	Matt. 18:32	cancelled
	tishbkoun	Matt. 18:35	cancel
shbegneen:		(see shbag)	
shbkat:		(see shbag)	
shbook:		imperative of shbag (see shbag)	
sheedii:	noun plural	The term is allied with devanii (Matt. 8:28), demons, but whereas deva is essentially elemental, sheedii appears to describe a whole mind controlled by a deva.	
	sheedii	Matt. 7:22; 8:31	demonic minds
shlama:		tranquility, that peace which is under and in accordance with God's will	
	shlama	Matt. 5:9	peace of God
shmeya:		sky, heaven	
	shmeya	Matt. 5:12, 18	heaven
	shmeya	Matt. 6:20	heaven
	dashmeya	Matt. 8:20	in the sky
shma:		name; output, that which is produced by a person; hence doctrines of a	

		teacher; teachings; true teachings, truth (when referring to the teachings of Jesus)
	shmi	John 1:12	His teachings (see 'i)
	b-shme	John 14:26	through me (see 'e)
	shma	Matt. 13:14	truth
sholtana:	noun	authority, executive authority
	sholtana	John 1:12	power
	sholtana	Matt. 9:6, 8	authority
shrakha:		Matt. 5:15	lamp (see nohra)
shrara:		truth
	dashrara	John 1:9	complete truth
	shrara	John 1:17	absolute truth
	shrari	John 4:23	truth
	bashrara	John 4:24	as complete truth
	shrara	John 5:31	truth
	bashrarak	John 17:17	your truth
	shrara	John 18:37 (2)	truth
sibyan:		will, the control entity in the mind. The executive authority of the mind with which one controls his attitudes, his goals and cue controls.
	sibyana	John 1:13 (2)	the will
	sibyanee	John 5:30	my will
	sibyani	John 5:30	will of Him
	sibyanak	Matt. 6:10	Thy will
	sibyani	' Matt. 7:21	the will of
sibyanak:	sibyan plus -ak (see sibyan)
sibyanee:	sibyan plus -e (see sibyan)
sibyani:	sibyan plus -i (see sibyan)
snee:	verb	hate, usually of human. May also

		appear as a mind structure underlying the attitudes and behavior we describe as destructive; hatred usually of human beings.
	(vasnee)	Matt. 5:43 have hate
	nisnee	Matt. 6:24 will hate
ta:	verb	come, arrive
	dateed	Matt. 12:32 which is to come
-ta:	suffix	indicating a neural structure is lifted in function from a silent or latent state to an attitude of perceptible quality (appears as -ey in touveyhoun)
taalan:	verb	let, yield, allow
	taalan	Matt. 6:13 let us yield
tagir:	verb	merchandise gainfully
	ittagar	Matt. 25:16, 17 made a commercial gain
	ittagarat	Matt. 25:20 commercial gain added
	ittagrit	Matt. 25:22 commercial gain
tashlim:		fulfill (see emali)
	tashlim	Matt. 5:33 fulfill
tava, tav:		(see touv)
tavata:	noun	heavenly words, acts or deeds as indicated by subject
	tavata	Matt. 12:34, 35 (2) heavenly words
teed:	verb	(see ta)
teyboota:	touv plus -oota	(see touv)
tghor:		commit adultery. While the number of lawful wives was unrestricted in Galilee at the time of Jesus, inter-

		course outside of wedlock, for male or female, was called tghor.	
	tghor	Matt. 5:27	commit adultery
	tghor	Matt. 5:32	commits adultery
ti-, tit-:	prefix	second person, imperative; also that is	
	ti (dagil)	Matt. 5:33	be (deceiving)
	ti (shbkoun)	Matt. 6:14, 15	you (forgive)
	tit (khazi)	Matt. 6:18	will (be noticed)
	tit (doonoon)	Matt. 7:1	condemn
	tit (deenoon)	Matt. 7:1	shall (be condemned)
	tit (deenoun)	Matt. 7:2	you shall (be sentenced)
	tit (palagh)	Matt. 12:25	you (divide)
	tid (rakhim)	Matt. 22:37	you shall (love)
	ti (rkham)	Matt. 22:39	you shall (love)
tidagil:	ti- plus dagil	(see dagle)	
tidrakhim:	tit- plus rakhma		
		(see rakhma)	
tikhi:	ti- plus khayi	(see khayi)	
tipkeah:		Matt. 5:13	tasteless
tirkham:	ti- plus rakhma	(see rakhma)	
tishbkoun, tishbkoon:	ti- plus shbag plus -oun or -oon	(see shbag)	
titdeenoon:	tit- plus dena plus -oon	(see dena)	
titdeenoun:	tit- plus dena plus -oun	(see dena)	
titdoonoon:	tit- plus dena plus -oon	(see dena)	

titkhayib:	tit- plus	
	khayib	(see khayib)
titkhazi:	tit- plus khazi	(see khazi)
titpalagh:	tit- plus	
	aplagh	(see aplagh)
tizdak:	ti- plus zadik	(see zadik)
touveyhoun:	touv plus -ta	
	plus -houn	(see touv)
touv:	noun	A neural structure within the mind which is of heavenly dignity and function; a neural structure desired by the Creator for all human minds which makes available thoughts and actions in conformity with the will of a loving God for increased happiness and well-being.
	touveyhoun	Matt. 5:3, 4, 5, 6
		7, 8, 9, 10, 11 heavenly attitude
	touvii	Matt. 5:45 the heavenly
	tava	Matt. 12:35 heavenly
	touveykeen	Matt. 13:16 heavenly attitude
	tav	Matt. 18:8, 9 better
	touv	Matt. 18:31 sense of right
	tava	Matt. 25:21, 23 good
	teyboota	John 1:14, 16 (2), 17 judgment or action (usually rendered as "grace" from the Greek)
va-:	prefix	conjunction; and
	va (snee)	Matt. 5:43 and (have hate)
vanveyii:		Matt. 22:40 its prophets
(vasnee):	va- plus snee	(see snee and va-)

yadeen:	yadi plus -een	(see yadi)	
yadi:		know, comprehend, understand	
	yadi	John 1:10	know
	yadeen	John 4:22 (2)	you know
	yadi	Matt. 6:8	knows
yod:		smallest letter in Aramaic alphabet	
	yod	Matt. 5:18	letter
yoolpani:		recital of learning, delivery of wisdom	
	yoolpani	Matt. 7:28	wisdom
zadekii:		those with zadik (see zadik)	
zadekoota:	zadik plus		
	-oota	(see zadik)	

zadik: The principle element of this word is integrity or rectitude. In the text, it is rendered as holy or righteous, which, of course, includes integrity. One who is koodsha in all things. The whole group of neural structures of the mind underlying attitudes and behavior which is most holy and righteous.

	zadekoota	Matt. 6:33	holiness
	zadekii	Matt. 9:13	the holy
	tizdak	Matt. 12:37	will be your holiness
	zadekii	Matt. 13:17	holy ones
zanyota:		wantonness in women, harlotry	
	zanyota	Matt. 5:32	her wantonness
zirta		a dash or scratch of a pen	
	zirta	Matt. 5:18	stroke

THE REV. SADOOK DE MAR SHIMUN, B.A.B.D.
ARCHDEACON AND PASTOR
SAINT JOHN'S ASSYRIAN-AMERICAN APOSTOLIC CHURCH
1034 WEST SHERIDAN ROAD
CHICAGO, ILLINOIS, USA

TELEPHONE: AMBASSADOR 2-5502

June 7, 1965

The Codex Khabouris

A Preliminary Report
by
Sadook de Mar Shimun, B.A.B.D.

The Khabouris Codex is a Manuscript of the whole New Testament in Christian Aramaic, commonly called Syriac, and according to the canon prevalent in the Churches whose liturgical language still is. The Codex is in excellent preservation; there are only three (3) pages which were added, by way of correction, by a later Nestorian hand.

Description

The Manuscript is written on animal skin, and consists of 254 leaves (folios). They measure about 10" plus x 7". The writing is in black ink, now somewhat brownish, and is in one column of 29 lines to the page. Titles and subscriptions of books are in red ink, as

94

well as the names of the places where they were written. The handwriting is uniform and very skillful, evidently the work of one scribe. The Codex made up of quires, which are numbered, of ten leaves each (quinions), that is, of five unions or five pieces of vellum of a leaf on each side of the binding cord. Though the binding and cover are very old, they do not appear to be coeval with the Manuscript.

Contents

The Manuscript was written as a whole New Testament of the twenty-two books of the Oriental Canon, which excludes Revelation and four short Epistles (II Peter, II and III John, and Jude). The arrangement of the Oriental Canon follows thus:

Matthew	Galatians
Mark	Ephesians
Luke	Phillipians
John	Collossians
Acts	I. Thessalonians
James	II. Thessalonians
Peter	I. Timothy
I. John, Romans	II. Timothy
I. Corinthians	Titus
II. Corinthians	Philemon
	Hebrews

The text of the Manuscript consists of twenty-five quires, of ten leaves each, plus three leaves. In addition it has one leaf at the end, on which the scribe has written a resume of the subscriptions and titles. The quires are arranged in the following order:

Subscriptions

At the end of the Gospel of Matthew the following subscription appears, "here ends the preaching of Matthew the Apostle, which he preached (proclaimed) and spoke in Palestine; and now the preaching of his beatitude, Marcus, the Apostle."

"Now, it has ended the preaching of his beatitude, Marcus the Apostle, which is proclaimed Rumaeet (in the language of the Romans) in the city of Rome. Here now begins the Holy Gospel according to the preaching of Luke, the Apostle."

"Now ends the preaching of Luke, the Apostle, which he preached in Greek, in the great City of Alexandria, and now do I begin to write the Holy Gospel according to the preaching of John, the Apostle."

"Now, I have finished writing the Holy Gospel according to the preaching of John, the Apostle, which he uttered in Greek in Ephesus, the great metropolis of Asia. Now do I begin, with the help and power of Christ, to write the Acts of the Holy Apostles."

"Now, the Epistle of James, the brother of our Lord."

"The end of the Epistle of James, the brother of our Lord. Now the Epistle of Peter the Apostle."

"End of the Epistle of Peter the Apostle. Now the Epistle of John the Apostle."

"I have finished writing the Acts of their beatitude the Apostles; the three Catholic Epistles. Now do I begin to write the letter according to the Epistles of his beatitude Paulus, the Apostle; teacher and preacher to the Gentiles. First his Epistle to the Romans."

"Now ends the Epistle to the Romans. I am now writing the 1st Epistle to the Corinthians."

Similar subscription with regard to 2nd Corinthians and the rest.

Significance

The significance of the Codex should be based on the following factors, each of which is of supreme importance. Its colophon which ascribes it to the first decade of the 3rd century, makes it the oldest Syriac-Aramaic known to exist. Its complete text offers the scholars a source of information hereto-fore lacking in the Aramaic field. It offers two lines of exploration: comparison of what we now have for the Aramaic text, which commonly is called Pshitta, and comparison with the Greek.

As to the former, it should be remembered that the Syria-Aramaic Canon and text of the New Testament were already long established before the Christological disputes, which were then

97

smoldering, and finally erupted in the fifth century, first divided the so-called Nestorians and then the Monophysites. For both of these Churches, despite their other disagreements, which eventually led to divergences, had the same New Testament. Since, as this and other records show, the Aramaic New Testament like the Khabouris Codex could be written at an early date, as its colophon states. Because this Manuscript is our first such whole New Testament, with so early a colophon, it becomes invaluable beyond comparison as a primary source in text criticism. It should be born in mind the authority which its early date commands.

In connection with the Greek New Testament and its derivatives (Latin, English, etc.) the comparative study of the Aramaic pattern of thought, and idiom is of primary importance and further ranging. For it was His language as well as that of His disciples and the people to whom He proclaimed His teachings. Aramaic studies thus play a key role in the New Testament problems, many of which are hotly contested problems of understanding, interpretation, translation, transmission, etc. Whatever we can glean from such studies increases the value of the New Testament to us. The significance of the prime source which the Khabouris Codex offers scarcely needs to be pointed out.